EDWARD'S MENAGERIE

#edsanimals

ABOUT THE AUTHOR

Kerry Lord is the founder of TOFT, a dynamic British yarn brand specialising in luxury wools and approachable patterns. Initially established with a focus on fashion-led knitting kits, Kerry first created the first edition of this very popular *Edward's Menagerie* series of book in 2012, which has encouraged and taught thousands of people around the world to crochet for the first time.

Kerry enjoys collaborating and co-hosting ever-larger crochet events to bring people together that have TOFT in common, and introduce new people to the craft.

Find the videos recorded by Kerry to accompany these patterns on the TOFT YouTube channel.

BE SOCIAL

Follow Kerry on most social media channels using @toft_uk to see more of her adventures in crochet.

One of the most exciting things about crocheting is joining the active online community helping and inspiring each other every day in their shared hobby. Share your makes using the tag #edsanimals to join in.

www.toftuk.com

EDWARD'S MENAGERIE

Over 50 easy-to-make soft toy animal crochet patterns

Kerry Lord

DAVID & CHARLES

www.davidandcharles.com

CONTENTS

ABOUT THE AUTHOR 2
BE SOCIAL 2
INTRODUCTION 7
HOW TO USE THIS BOOK 8
YOU WILL NEED 10
SIZE OPTIONS 12
STANDARD FORMS 14

PATTERNS

LEVEL 1

EMMA the Bunny 18
ALEXANDRE the Russian Blue Cat 20
PIOTR the Polar Bear 22
BRIDGET the Elephant 24
RICHARD the Large White Pig 26
MILO the Dog 28
GEORGINA the Hippo 30
AUSTIN the Rhino 32
KARL the Wallaby 34
SIMON the Sheep 36
RUFUS the Lion 38
BENEDICT the Chimpanzee 40
WINSTON the Aardvark 42
GERMAINE the Gorilla 44
ISAAC the American Bison 46

LEVEL 2

PENELOPE the Bear 50
HANK the Dorset Down Sheep 52
FIONA the Panda 54
ANGHARAD the Donkey 56
DOUGLAS the Highland Cow 58
LAURENCE the Tiger 60
CHARDONNAY the Palomino Pony 62
ALICE the Zebra 64
AUDREY the Nanny Goat 66
BETH the Dutch Rabbit 68
ANDREW the Sea Otter 70
OWEN the Wildebeest 72
CLARENCE the Bat 74
FRANCIS the Hedgehog 76

LEVEL 3

SAMUEL the Koala	80
WILLIAM the Sloth Bear	82
BRADLEE the Grey Squirrel	84
CASPAR the Peary Caribou	86
SARAH the Friesian Cow	88
CAITLIN the Giraffe	90
ESME the Fox	92
BLAKE the Orangutan	94
HAMLET the Cheetah	96
JESSIE the Raccoon	98
NOAH the Zwartbles Sheep	100
CHRISTOPHE the Wolf	102
NATASHA the Two-Toed Sloth	104
NOUSHA the Persian Cat	106
PERRY the Guinea Pig	108
CYBIL the Sugar Glider	110
NOEL the Chipmunk	112
GINA the Hyena	114
ANDREA the Ocelot	118
SAVANNA the African Painted Dog	122
JANE the Pangolin	126

TECHNICALS

BASIC SKILLS	130
ABBREVIATIONS	131
WORKING THE STITCHES	132
FINISHING TECHNIQUES	135
ADDITIONAL TECHNIQUES	136
TOPKNOTS AND TAILS	137
STUFFING AND SEWING	138
FACE DETAILS	140
WASHING AND SAFETY	141
THANK YOU	142
SUPPLIERS	142

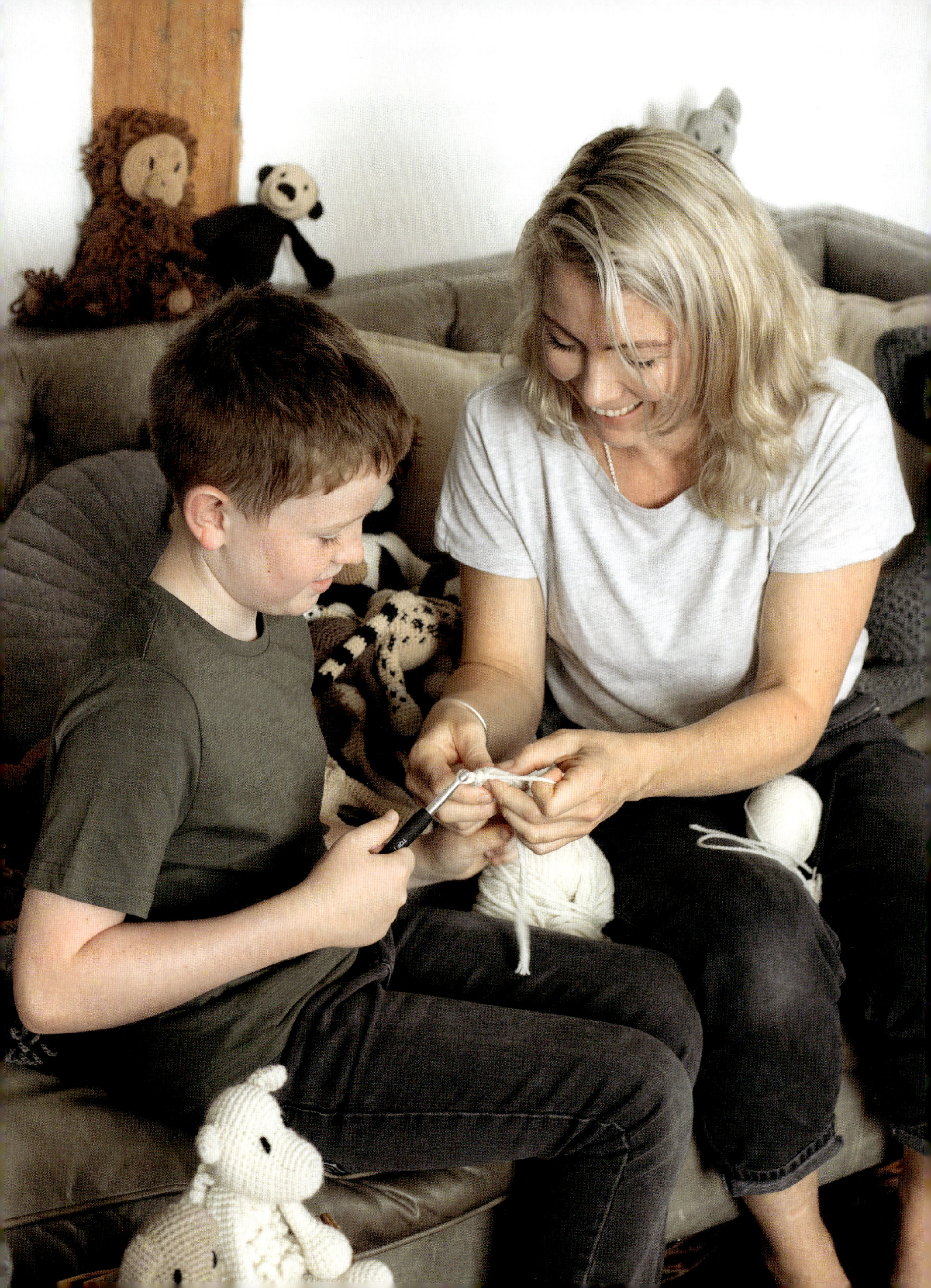

INTRODUCTION

Edward's Menagerie has now been a part of my life for over a decade, and has taken me on adventures around the world I could never have imagined when writing this book the first time. Along the way I have met tens of thousands of people who have enjoyed crocheting these animals just as much as I do, and with them I have shared in stories of how much these patterns have spread joy, triumph and pride at life's most challenging moments.

With this ten-year edition I have added everything I have learned over that decade teaching more and more people to crochet, and the patterns have become even easier for a beginner crocheter to pick them up and begin making. Step-by-step techniques have been included at the back of the book for the stitches used, so, even if you have never tried crochet before, you will be able to get started straight away.

It was shortly before my 40-week due date that I first picked up a crochet hook. Since then, I have shelved my knitting needles and not looked back. In the 14 days in which Edward kept me waiting, 14 animals were made (albeit several were inside out and I still had little idea how to write down what I had done!). In my first six months as a new mum with an expanding yarn business I only managed to add a few more animals to the mantlepiece. It was really only once I was living with a baby who wanted to interact and play with my creations that a new wave of enthusiasm took hold of me. I now live with a pre-teen Edward and a daughter and have gone on to crochet a few stitches very nearly every day since he was born, resulting in far more animals than even the biggest zoo.

Bridget the Elephant was the first animal to arrive in Edward's nursery, and she remains one of the simplest patterns, along with *Alexandre the Russian Blue Cat* and *Emma the Bunny*. If you are a beginner, I would recommend working your way up to the likes of the loop stitches on *Blake the Orangutan* and colour changing on *Hamlet the Cheetah*, as these patterns are a little more complex. This ten-year edition includes new patterns and techniques for designs I could not have begun to conceive of when I first learned to crochet, but that I know you will love developing your skills with beyond the double crochet stitch.

The patterns for *Edward's Menagerie* are designed for you and your friends and family to enjoy and are for private use only. I can't wait to see photos of your menagerie animals; make sure you share them using the hashtag **#edsanimals**, so myself and the rest of the incredibly creative TOFT community can find them.

Enjoy,

Kerry

HOW TO USE THIS BOOK

Edward's Menagerie has been divided into three levels to indicate how many techniques are used in the making of that animal. I would like to emphasise that you do not need a degree in anything to make a Level 3 animal. I would, however, suggest that you maybe try a Level 1 or 2 animal first if you are totally new to crochet.

LEVEL 1

Animals using one colour and only chain, slip stitch and double crochet.

LEVEL 2

Animals for which you need to do basic colour changing. Instructions for this can be found in the *Technicals* section.

LEVEL 3

Animals that require more complex colour changing and those that require the loop stitch. Again, instructions for this can be found in the *Technicals* section.

The animals in *Edward's Menagerie* are a family and thus share common body shapes. You will need to refer to the *Standard Forms* page when making any of the animals in this book. You will notice that this page has a grey edge to help you find it quickly as you are working through the pattern. After you have made one animal, you will pick up the pattern quickly (and become very familiar with your six times table!).

To keep each pattern simple and concise, I have omitted the stuffing and sewing-up instructions, as these are common to all. Please refer to the *Stuffing and Sewing* pages in the *Technicals* section before you start, so that you are aware of the correct order and place in the pattern to do this.

The patterns all use British crochet terminology and common crochet abbreviations. US conversions and full explanations can be found in the *Technicals* section.

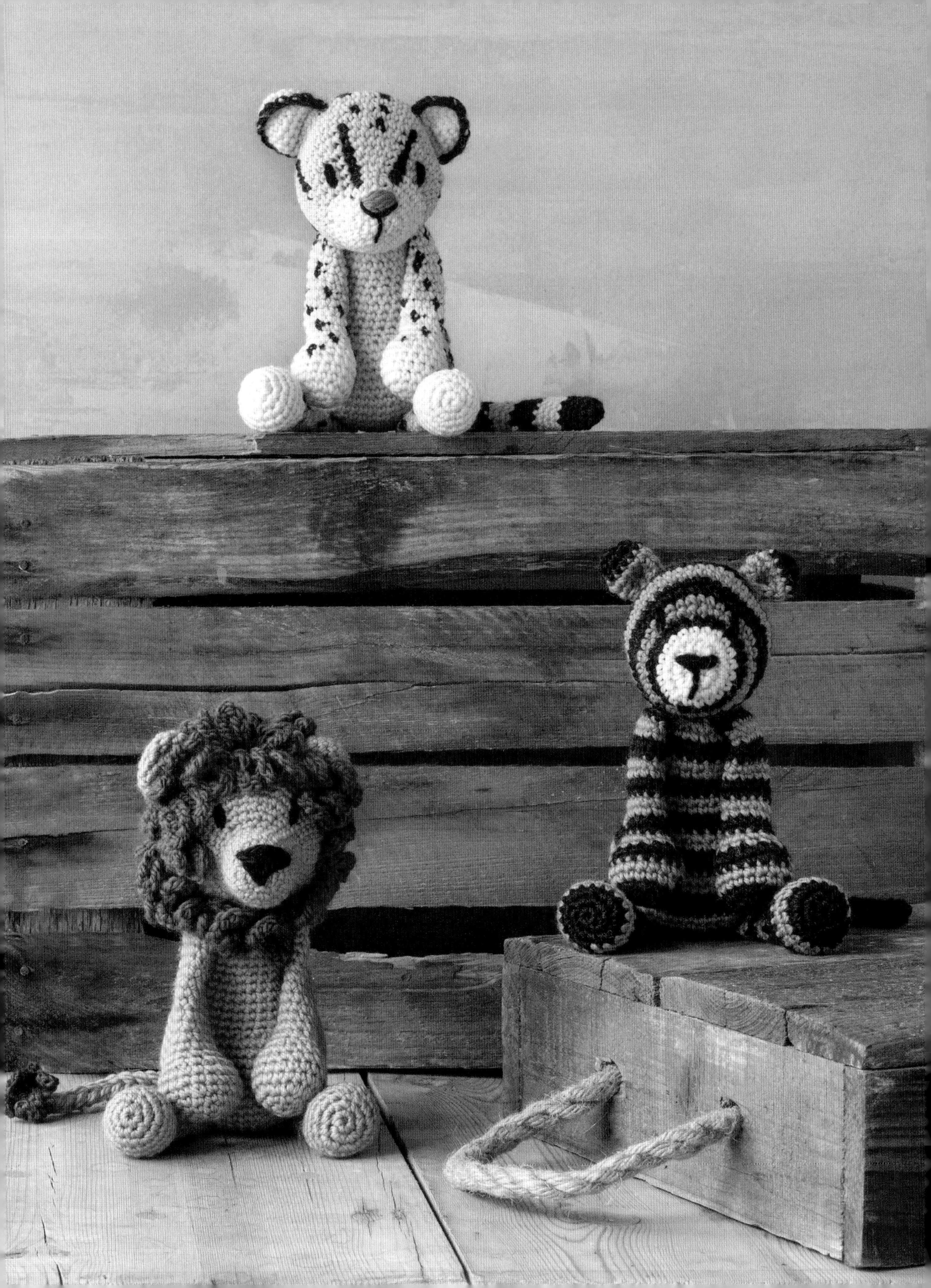

YOU WILL NEED

MY YARN CHOICE

The *Edward's Menagerie* animals on each of the project pages of this book have been crocheted in a TOFT pure wool Double Knitting (DK) weight yarn on a 3mm hook. This collection of animal patterns showcases the soft handle of natural fibres, the depth and range of natural colours and the tactile appeal of the resulting fabric. The creation of *Edward's Menagerie* was driven by an intimate knowledge and understanding of TOFT yarn. Naturally, I recommend using TOFT yarn to guarantee that your animals look just like mine, but the patterns will work in any other non-fancy spun yarn. The resulting animals will vary drastically should you choose to work up an elephant in blue acrylic yarn, or a lion in yellow cotton, but the patterns will work if you match your hook size to your yarn and check that your tension makes a dense, crisp fabric.

YARN COLOURS

The animals in this book have been made using a palette of 12 natural colours. These subtle shades of creams, browns and greys provide all you need. The colour recommendations depicted are not fixed rules. The beauty of the spectrum of natural yarn is not only that it is 'animal' coloured, but also that each yarn colour is interchangeable with a myriad of substitutes. My advice on selecting colours would be not to spend too long staring at images on a computer, but to use your instincts and your mind's eye to achieve the best results.

Some animals use only one colour, others two, and a handful combine three for a more detailed finish. The colours and quantity you will need in TOFT DK yarn to create the standard size of animal is stated at the start of every pattern.

MATERIALS FOR STUFFING

On the whole I have chosen to stuff the animals with a premium recycled polyester toy stuffing. If you are making these animals for children then a synthetic filling may be the most practical option as it makes the animals fully hand-washable. However, I do often use pure wool and plant-based cotton and kapok stuffing when making the animals for adults to enjoy as mascots in their homes or at work as an all-natural environmental choice.

MATERIALS FOR FACES

I have used black yarn to sew on all the animals' eyes and nostrils. Using a dyed yarn or embroidery thread will give you a lovely contrast with the natural colours of the yarn, and the eyes will really stand out with a glint from the fabric. Alternatively, you could use buttons, beads or safety eyes if you wish, adding these in before you do final sewing up. Do not use safety eyes, buttons, beads or glass eyes on toys intended for children under three years old as they are a potential choking hazard; securely embroider the features instead as I have done so.

TO MAKE JUST ONE, OR INDEED ALL, OF THE ANIMALS IN THIS BOOK, THE REQUIREMENTS LIST IS THE SAME:

Yarn in appropriate colours and quantities (see *Size Options* and each project)

One hook in an appropriate size to the yarn being used (see *Size Options*)

A scrap of yarn or stitch marker to keep track of your progress

Stuffing material

Black contrast yarn for face details

Scissors

Sewing needle

COLOURS OPPOSITE (from top left)

Cream, Oatmeal, Stone, Silver, Shale, Steel, Camel, Fudge, Chestnut, Mushroom, Cocoa, Charcoal

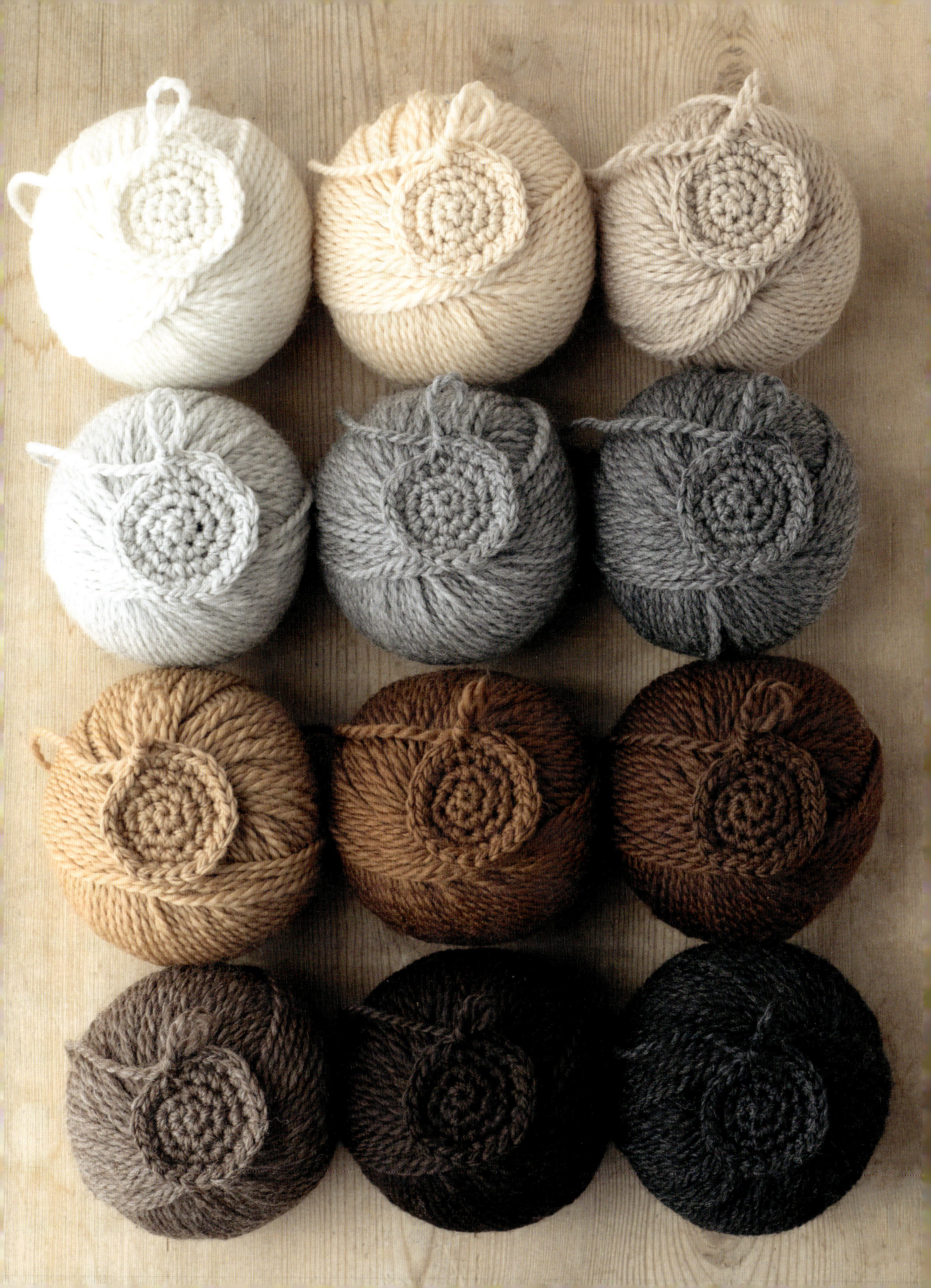

SIZE OPTIONS

The standard-sized *Edward's Menagerie* animal shown on each project page is worked in TOFT pure wool Double Knitting (DK) weight yarn on a 3mm crochet hook (for US crocheters: light worsted/8ply yarn on a C2 or D3 hook). The beauty of the pattern is that you never need to change the hook size and you need only one tool to make all 50 animals in this book!

All the figures given here are approximate and based on my experience in working with TOFT yarns. You could make any one of these animals in any thickness of yarn, but with the Level 3 animals you may find some parts become quite demanding when worked in very fine yarns. Thicker yarns and bigger hooks often suit beginners best, as it can be less fiddly and is easier to see the stitches.

You can always supersize your project by crocheting with multiple strands of yarn held together as you work the stitches. In TOFT yarn two strands of Fine equals a DK, two strands of DK an Aran and two strands of Aran a Chunky: so you can even hold four strands of DK together to create a giant animal!

Yarn quantities are based on using TOFT pure wool yarn. If you use another brand, the quantities required may vary significantly depending on the composition of the yarn.

Animals that use the loop stitch or chain loops to add details such as manes or topknots will take considerably more yarn than others.

Your hook size needs to be selected based on yarn thickness but also considering your own personal tension. Adjust your hook size to accommodate your tension and thickness of yarn ensuring that your fabric is dense: if it is too loose your stuffing will show through; if it is too tight your animals will be stiff and hard to work.

SMALL

YARN WEIGHT	UK	FINE (half a strand of DK)
	US/AU	SPORT/4PLY
QUANTITY	G	20-30
	OZ	¾-1
HOOK SIZE	MM	2
	US/AU	A
FINISHED SIZE	CM	10
	IN	4
TENSION	CM	2 x 2cm = 7 sts x 8 rnds
	IN	¾ x ¾in = 7 sts x 8 rnds

STANDARD

YARN WEIGHT	UK	DK
	US/AU	LIGHT WORSTED/8PLY
QUANTITY	G	60-100
	OZ	2-3½
HOOK SIZE	MM	3
	US/AU	C2/D3
FINISHED SIZE	CM	18
	IN	7
TENSION	CM	3 x 3cm = 6 sts x 7 rnds
	IN	1¼ x 1¼in = 6 sts x 7 rnds

The tension measurements below are approximate and measured over standard double crochet stitches worked in a spiral. See *Technicals* for more information.

The finished sizes shown here relate to an animal when in a sitting position measured from its bottom to the top of its head – all ears, horns and manes are additional to this.

INTERNATIONAL TERMS

I have used British English crochet terms throughout. 'Double crochet' (dc) is the same as the American English 'single crochet' (sc). For clarification on which stitch this refers to and for any additional abbreviations, see the instructions in the *Technicals* section.

LARGE			
YARN WEIGHT	UK	ARAN (2 strands of DK)	
	US/AU	WORSTED/10PLY	
QUANTITY	G	200-400	
	OZ	7-14	
HOOK SIZE	MM	5	
	US/AU	H8	
FINISHED SIZE	CM	24	
	IN	9½	
TENSION	CM	5 x 5cm = 6 sts x 7 rnds	
	IN	2 x 2in = 6 sts x 7 rnds	

GIANT			
YARN WEIGHT	UK	CHUNKY (4 strands of DK)	
	US/AU	BULKY/12PLY	
QUANTITY	G	600-1000	
	OZ	20-35	
HOOK SIZE	MM	8	
	US/AU	L11	
FINISHED SIZE	CM	34	
	IN	13½	
TENSION	CM	7 x 7cm = 6 sts x 7 rnds	
	IN	2¾ x 2¾in = 6 sts x 7 rnds	

STANDARD FORMS

The majority of pieces are created using a standard increase of adding six stitches evenly into each round to create a flat hexagonal piece of crochet, worked in a spiral from the centre outwards. This forms the base of all the bodies and the feet, and the backs of the heads which then become three dimensional once you stop increasing. The body and legs are worked from the base upwards and all heads are worked from the back forwards.

When you have completed a part, unless it is otherwise stated, break the yarn leaving at least 20cm (8in) with which you can sew up and pull it off the hook. I choose to stuff all parts once I have completed crocheting them, and so there is no need to do this as you go along unless it is stated in the pattern before decreasing to a pointed finish. See also *Stuffing and Sewing* and *Topknots and Tails* in *Technicals* for further advice on this.

For a more detailed explanation of the techniques, including how to start, how to work the stitches and changing colours, please refer to the *Technicals* section.

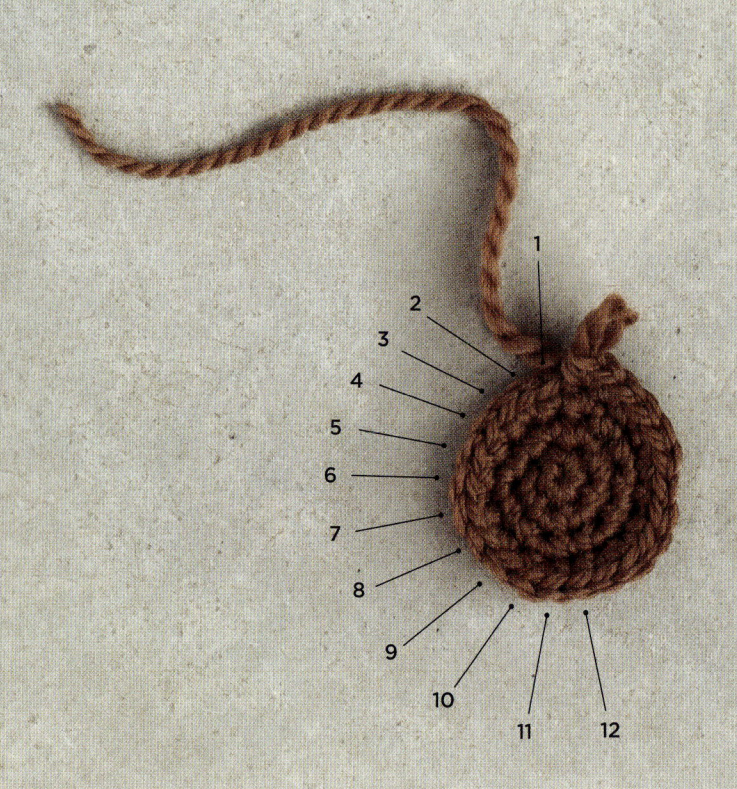

COUNTING

A basic skill to get yourself out of trouble is counting the number of stitches at the end of a round. After each round involving decreasing or increasing instructions, the number at the end in brackets will indicate how many stitches you should now have to work with. If you complete a round and this number is incorrect, simply pull back the round to your marker on the previous round and rework it.

STANDARD LEGS

Begin by dc6 into ring (see *Technicals*)
Rnd 1 (dc2 into next st) 6 times (12)
Rnd 2 (dc1, dc2 into next st) 6 times (18)
Rnds 3-6 dc (4 rnds)
Rnd 7 (dc1, dc2tog) 6 times (12)
Rnds 8-22 dc (15 rnds)

Stuff the ends only and then fold flat and sew or dc through both sides of rnd across the top to close (see *Finishing the Feet and Legs* under *Stuffing and Sewing* in the *Technicals* section).

STANDARD BODY

Begin by dc6 into ring (see *Technicals*)
Rnd 1 (dc2 into next st) 6 times (12)
Rnd 2 (dc1, dc2 into next st) 6 times (18)
Rnd 3 (dc2, dc2 into next st) 6 times (24)
Rnd 4 (dc3, dc2 into next st) 6 times (30)
Rnd 5 (dc4, dc2 into next st) 6 times (36)
Rnd 6 (dc5, dc2 into next st) 6 times (42)
Rnd 7 (dc6, dc2 into next st) 6 times (48)
Rnds 8-12 dc (5 rnds)
Rnd 13 dc13, (dc4, dc2tog) 3 times, dc17 (45)
Rnd 14 dc
Rnd 15 (dc1, dc2tog) 15 times (30)
Rnds 16-20 dc (5 rnds)
Rnd 21 (dc3, dc2tog) 6 times (24)
Rnds 22-26 dc (5 rnds)
Rnd 27 (dc2, dc2tog) 6 times (18)
Rnd 28 dc
Rnd 29 (dc2tog) 9 times (9)

Break yarn leaving a long length with which to sew the head to the body then stuff and gather remaining stitches to close.

TIP: Marking the centre of the body to help with symmetry when sewing up can be done by placing a marker into the second decrease of round 13.

STANDARD FORMS

LEVEL 1

The animals in Level 1 are a great way to learn the basics of crochet. They are suitable for complete beginners who use the *Technicals* section to learn.

EMMA the Bunny

ALEXANDRE the Russian Blue Cat

PIOTR the Polar Bear

BRIDGET the Elephant

RICHARD the Large White Pig

MILO the Dog

GEORGINA the Hippo

AUSTIN the Rhino

KARL the Wallaby

SIMON the Sheep

RUFUS the Lion

BENEDICT the Chimpanzee

WINSTON the Aardvark

GERMAINE the Gorilla

ISAAC the American Bison

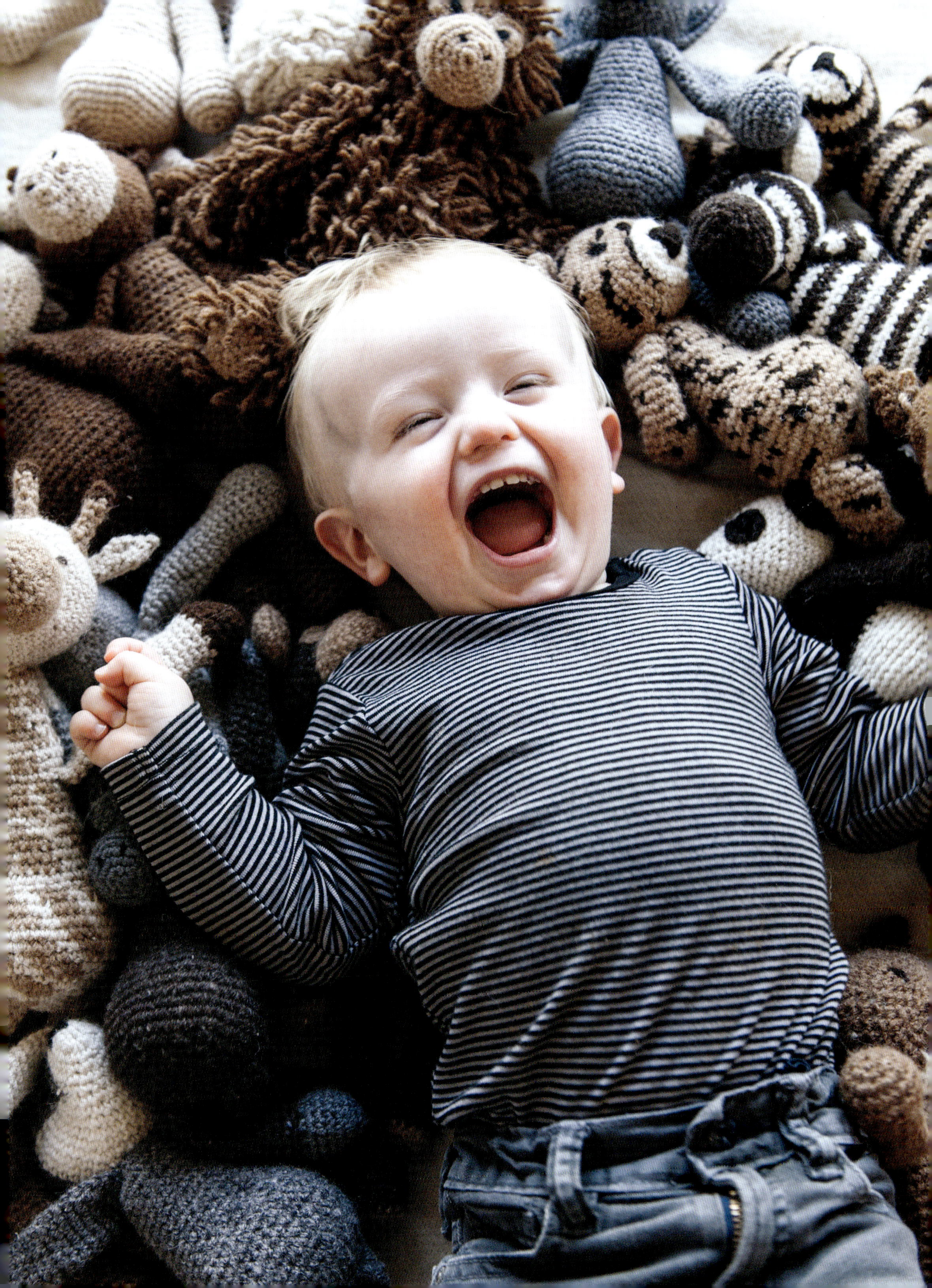

EMMA
the Bunny

Emma is an extremely lovable bunny whose aura is kept in balance by regular dates with her yoga mat. She's a very house-proud mummy rabbit and her warren is her sanctuary. Although often reluctant to tie up her ears and get on with the housework, she does a very fine job once she sets her mind to it. Her creative talents have long slept dormant while other people have become her priority, but it looks as if that might be about to change. Once there's a vase of fresh flowers and a pot of Earl Grey tea brewing on the side, it's time for Emma to get out her needles and create.

YARN REQUIRED

75g TOFT DK yarn Stone
Length of Mushroom for nose

See also: *You Will Need* and *Size Options*.

LEGS (make four)
Work as STANDARD in Stone

BODY
Work as STANDARD in Stone

HEAD
Begin by dc6 into ring
Rnd 1 (dc2 into next st) 6 times (12)
Rnd 2 (dc1, dc2 into next st) 6 times (18)
Rnd 3 (dc2, dc2 into next st) 6 times (24)
Rnd 4 (dc3, dc2 into next st) 6 times (30)
Rnd 5 (dc4, dc2 into next st) 6 times (36)
Rnd 6 (dc5, dc2 into next st) 6 times (42)
Rnds 7-11 dc (5 rnds)
Rnd 12 (dc5, dc2tog) 6 times (36)
Rnd 13 dc
Rnd 14 (dc4, dc2tog) 3 times, dc18 (33)
Rnd 15 (dc3, dc2tog) 3 times, dc18 (30)
Rnd 16 dc
Rnd 17 (dc3, dc2tog) 6 times (24)
Rnd 18 dc12, (dc1, dc2tog) 4 times (20)
Rnd 19 (dc2, dc2tog) 5 times (15)
Rnd 20 (dc2tog) 7 times, dc1 (8)
Stuff and gather remaining stitches to close.

EARS (make two)
Begin by dc6 into ring
Rnd 1 (dc1, dc2 into next st) 3 times (9)
Rnds 2-3 dc (2 rnds)
Rnd 4 (dc2, dc2 into next st) 3 times (12)
Rnd 5 dc
Rnd 6 (dc3, dc2 into next st) 3 times (15)
Rnd 7 (dc2, dc2 into next st) 5 times (20)
Rnds 8-13 dc (6 rnds)
Rnd 14 (dc3, dc2tog) 4 times (16)
Rnds 15-16 dc (2 rnds)
Rnd 17 (dc6, dc2tog) twice (14)
Rnds 18-22 dc (5 rnds)
Rnd 23 (dc5, dc2tog) twice (12)
Rnds 24-30 dc (7 rnds)
Do not stuff. Fold flat and sew or dc through both sides of rnd to close.

TAIL
Begin by dc6 into ring
Rnd 1 (dc2 into next st) 6 times (12)
Rnd 2 (dc1, dc2 into next st) 6 times (18)
Rnds 3-6 dc (4 rnds)
Rnd 7 (dc1, dc2tog) 6 times (12)
Rnd 8 (dc2tog) 6 times (6)
Stuff and gather remaining stitches to close.

Finish by sewing eyes into place with Black yarn and nose with Mushroom yarn.

LEVEL 1 EMMA THE BUNNY

ALEXANDRE
the Russian Blue Cat

Lex is convinced that he's one cool cat. He has spent most of the last three years of his life torturing his mother by partaking in the latest fashion trends. He is a self-proclaimed expert in everything a modern teenage boy should be, most notably in the maintenance of his social media profile and taking the best selfie. He is looking forward to learning to drive soon – not because he longs for adventure, but so he no longer has to have his style cramped by the bus. Who knows what the careers advisor might recommend for his future?

YARN REQUIRED

75g TOFT DK yarn Silver

See also: *You Will Need* and *Size Options*.

LEGS (make four)
Work as STANDARD in Silver

BODY
Work as STANDARD in Silver

HEAD
Begin by dc6 into ring
Rnd 1 (dc2 into next st) 6 times (12)
Rnd 2 (dc1, dc2 into next st) 6 times (18)
Rnd 3 (dc2, dc2 into next st) 6 times (24)
Rnd 4 (dc3, dc2 into next st) 6 times (30)
Rnd 5 (dc4, dc2 into next st) 6 times (36)
Rnd 6 (dc5, dc2 into next st) 6 times (42)
Rnds 7-11 dc (5 rnds)
Rnd 12 (dc5, dc2tog) 6 times (36)
Rnd 13 (dc4, dc2tog) 6 times (30)
Rnd 14 (dc3, dc2tog) 6 times (24)
Rnd 15 dc
Rnd 16 (dc1, dc2tog) 8 times (16)
Rnd 17 dc
Rnd 18 (dc2, dc2tog) 4 times (12)
Rnd 19 (dc2, dc2tog) 3 times (9)
Rnd 20 (dc1, dc2tog) 3 times (6)
Stuff and gather remaining stitches to close.

EARS (make two)
Begin by dc5 into ring
Rnd 1 (dc2 into next st) 5 times (10)
Rnd 2 dc
Rnd 3 (dc2 into next st) 10 times (20)
Rnds 4-5 dc (2 rnds)
Rnd 6 (dc8, dc2tog) twice (18)
Rnd 7 (dc7, dc2tog) twice (16)
Rnd 8 dc
Rnd 9 (dc6, dc2tog) twice (14)
Rnd 10 (dc5, dc2tog) twice (12)
Rnd 11 (dc4, dc2tog) twice (10)
Rnd 12 (dc3, dc2tog) twice (8)
Rnd 13 (dc2, dc2tog) twice (6)
Do not stuff. Gather remaining stitches to close.

TAIL
Begin by dc6 into ring
Rnds 1-26 dc (26 rnds)
Do not stuff.

Finish by sewing eyes and nose into place with Black yarn.

LEVEL 1 ALEXANDRE THE RUSSIAN BLUE CAT

21

PIOTR
the Polar Bear

Piotr landed the job of his dreams straight out of university. His career as a computer games tester has gone from strength to strength, fuelled by a fast-food diet that is delivered straight to his door. He works from the luxury of his attic in a modest house where the heating is on full-blast all year round, for he really feels the cold. Piotr is kept blindingly white due to his utter aversion to sunshine and not often finding a need to venture out into it. He is one of the best at what he does and is turning the heads that matter, but despite this bear's dedication to his work he still finds time to call his grandma every other day and check how warm her feet are.

YARN REQUIRED

75g TOFT DK yarn Cream

See also: *You Will Need* and *Size Options*.

LEGS (make four)
Work as STANDARD in Cream

BODY
Work as STANDARD in Cream

HEAD
Begin by dc6 into ring
Rnd 1 (dc2 into next st) 6 times (12)
Rnd 2 (dc1, dc2 into next st) 6 times (18)
Rnd 3 (dc2, dc2 into next st) 6 times (24)
Rnd 4 (dc3, dc2 into next st) 6 times (30)
Rnd 5 (dc4, dc2 into next st) 6 times (36)
Rnd 6 (dc5, dc2 into next st) 6 times (42)
Rnds 7-11 dc (5 rnds)
Rnd 12 (dc5, dc2tog) 6 times (36)
Rnds 13-15 dc (3 rnds)
Rnd 16 dc10, (dc2, dc2tog) 4 times, dc10 (32)
Rnd 17 dc8, (dc2, dc2tog) 4 times, dc8 (28)
Rnd 18 dc6, (dc2, dc2tog) 4 times, dc6 (24)
Rnd 19 dc4, (dc2, dc2tog) 4 times, dc4 (20)
Rnd 20 dc4, (dc1, dc2tog) 4 times, dc4 (16)
Rnd 21 dc
Rnd 22 dc4, (dc2tog) 4 times, dc4 (12)
Rnd 23 (dc2tog) 6 times (6)
Stuff and gather remaining stitches to close.

EARS (make two)
Begin by dc6 into ring
Rnd 1 (dc2 into next st) 6 times (12)
Rnds 2-5 dc (4 rnds)
Rnd 6 (dc2tog) 6 times (6)
Do not stuff. Gather remaining stitches to close.

TAIL
Begin by dc6 into ring
Rnd 1 (dc2 into next st) 6 times (12)
Rnds 2-3 dc (2 rnds)
Rnd 4 (dc2tog) 6 times (6)
Rnd 5 (dc2tog) 3 times (3)
Do not stuff.

Finish by sewing eyes and nose into place with Black yarn.

LEVEL 1 THE POLAR BEAR

BRIDGET
the Elephant

Bridget has a sweet tooth. More than anything else in the world she loves baking cakes, and scones, and cookies and more cakes... but especially custard tarts. As a young elephant she would spend hours having tea parties with her dolls and she never really grew out of it. Nowadays, her idea of the best party is a baby shower: the glory of baking the best cake, no pressure to swap her cup and saucer for a wine glass, and lots and lots of baby chat.

YARN REQUIRED

75g TOFT DK yarn Steel

See also: *You Will Need* and *Size Options*.

LEGS (make four)
Begin by dc6 into ring
Rnd 1 (dc2 into next st) 6 times (12)
Rnd 2 (dc1, dc2 into next st) 6 times (18)
Rnd 3 (dc2, dc2 into next st) 6 times (24)
Rnds 4-6 dc (3 rnds)
Rnd 7 (dc1, dc2tog) 8 times (16)
Rnd 8 (dc2, dc2tog) 4 times (12)
Rnds 9-24 dc (16 rnds)
Stuff the ends only and then fold flat and sew or dc through both sides of rnd across the top to close.

BODY
Work as STANDARD in Steel

HEAD
Begin by dc6 into ring
Rnd 1 (dc2 into next st) 6 times (12)
Rnd 2 (dc1, dc2 into next st) 6 times (18)
Rnd 3 (dc2, dc2 into next st) 6 times (24)
Rnd 4 (dc3, dc2 into next st) 6 times (30)
Rnd 5 (dc4, dc2 into next st) 6 times (36)
Rnd 6 (dc5, dc2 into next st) 6 times (42)
Rnds 7-11 dc (5 rnds)
Rnd 12 (dc5, dc2tog) 6 times (36)
Rnd 13 dc
Rnd 14 (dc4, dc2tog) 3 times, dc18 (33)
Rnd 15 (dc3, dc2tog) 3 times, dc18 (30)
Rnd 16 dc
Rnd 17 (dc3, dc2tog) 6 times (24)
Rnd 18 dc12, (dc1, dc2tog) 4 times (20)
Rnd 19 (dc2, dc2tog) 5 times (15)
Rnds 20-22 dc (3 rnds)
Rnd 23 (dc1, dc2tog) 5 times (10)
Rnds 24-33 dc (10 rnds)
Stuff and sew flat across end of trunk to close.

EARS (make two)
Begin by dc6 into ring
Rnd 1 (dc2 into next st) 6 times (12)
Rnd 2 (dc1, dc2 into next st) 6 times (18)
Rnd 3 (dc2, dc2 into next st) 6 times (24)
Rnd 4 (dc3, dc2 into next st) 6 times (30)
Rnd 5 (dc4, dc2 into next st) 6 times (36)
Rnd 6 (dc5, dc2 into next st) 6 times (42)
Rnd 7 (dc6, dc2 into next st) 6 times (48)
Fold in half and dc through both sides of rnd around the edge to close.

TAIL
Create CHAIN TAIL: using four strands of yarn held together, ch6 sts with this oversized yarn then work three ch10 CHAIN LOOPS onto the end using a single strand (see *Technicals*)

Finish by sewing eyes into place with Black yarn.

LEVEL 1 BRIDGET THE ELEPHANT

25

RICHARD
the Large White Pig

Richard does not have a mobile phone. He is a neo-Luddite rooted firmly in his allotment, reading the daily newspaper from the back page forwards. He was once quite a soccer player, but hung up his studs for slippers just before the glamour arrived in the business. The internet remains a mystery to him despite countless well-meaning grandchildren enrolling him on courses and classes. His great-grandchildren love their 'GGpig' and his funny ways, and still fear going in goal against the golden trotter.

YARN REQUIRED

75g TOFT DK yarn Oatmeal

See also: *You Will Need* and *Size Options*.

LEGS (make four)
Work as STANDARD in Oatmeal

BODY
Work as STANDARD in Oatmeal

HEAD
Begin by dc6 into ring
Rnd 1 (dc2 into next st) 6 times (12)
Rnd 2 (dc1, dc2 into next st) 6 times (18)
Rnd 3 (dc2, dc2 into next st) 6 times (24)
Rnd 4 (dc3, dc2 into next st) 6 times (30)
Rnd 5 (dc4, dc2 into next st) 6 times (36)
Rnd 6 (dc5, dc2 in next st) 6 times (42)
Rnds 7-11 dc (5 rnds)
Rnd 12 (dc5, dc2tog) 6 times (36)
Rnd 13 dc
Rnd 14 (dc4, dc2tog) 3 times, dc18 (33)
Rnd 15 (dc3, dc2tog) 3 times, dc18 (30)
Rnd 16 dc
Rnd 17 (dc3, dc2tog) 6 times (24)
Rnd 18 dc12, (dc1, dc2tog) 4 times (20)
Rnd 19 (dc2, dc2tog) 5 times (15)
Rnds 20-21 dc (2 rnds)
Rnd 22 (dc2 into next st, dc4) 3 times (18)

SNOUT END
Begin by dc6 into ring
Rnd 1 (dc2 into next st) 6 times (12)
Rnd 2 (dc1, dc2 into next st) 6 times (18)
Stuff head and join end onto final round of head with a round of dc from the front through both sets of stitches.

EARS (make two)
Begin by dc6 into ring
Rnd 1 (dc2 into next st) 6 times (12)
Rnd 2 (dc1, dc2 into next st) 6 times (18)
Rnd 3 (dc2, dc2 into next st) 6 times (24)
Rnd 4 (dc3, dc2 into next st) 6 times (30)
Rnd 5 (dc4, dc2 into next st) 6 times (36)
Rnd 6 (dc5, dc2 in next st) 6 times (42)
Fold ears in half and dc10 through both sides, leaving remaining stitches unworked.

TAIL
Sl st into tail position
Ch10, turn and dc2 into every stitch back down chain (20)

Finish by sewing eyes and nostrils into place with Black yarn.

LEVEL 1 RICHARD THE LARGE WHITE PIG

MILO
the Dog

Milo's a nearly fully grown puppy looking for love anywhere and everywhere he can get his nose stuck into. With his little tail wagging and his big ears pricked he bounds into every situation with his heart wide open and tongue hanging out. This young pup is overdue a bit of good luck having lived through some hard times despite being so young. Hopefully a change of fate is on the way and his pot of gold and Prince Charming are just around the next corner.

YARN REQUIRED

75g TOFT DK yarn Fudge
Length of Cocoa for nose

See also: *You Will Need* and *Size Options*.

LEGS (make four)
Work as STANDARD in Fudge

BODY
Work as STANDARD in Fudge

HEAD
Begin by dc6 into ring
Rnd 1 (dc2 into next st) 6 times (12)
Rnd 2 (dc1, dc2 into next st) 6 times (18)
Rnd 3 (dc2, dc2 into next st) 6 times (24)
Rnd 4 (dc3, dc2 into next st) 6 times (30)
Rnd 5 (dc4, dc2 into next st) 6 times (36)
Rnd 6 (dc5, dc2 into next st) 6 times (42)
Rnds 7-12 dc (6 rnds)
Rnd 13 (dc5, dc2tog) 6 times (36)
Rnd 14 (dc4, dc2tog) 6 times (30)
Rnd 15 (dc1, dc2tog) 10 times (20)
Rnds 16-20 dc (5 rnds)
Rnd 21 (dc2tog, dc1, dc2tog) 4 times (12)
Rnd 22 (dc2, dc2tog) 3 times (9)
Stuff and gather remaining stitches to close.

EARS (make two)
Begin by dc6 into ring
Rnd 1 (dc1, dc2 into next st) 3 times (9)
Rnd 2 (dc2, dc2 into next st) 3 times (12)
Rnds 3-4 dc (2 rnds)
Rnd 5 (dc3, dc2 into next st) 3 times (15)
Rnd 6 dc
Rnd 7 (dc4, dc2 into next st) 3 times (18)
Rnd 8 dc
Rnd 9 (dc5, dc2 into next st) 3 times (21)
Rnds 10-11 dc (2 rnds)
Rnd 12 (dc1, dc2tog) 7 times (14)
Rnd 13 (dc2tog) 7 times (7)
Do not stuff. Gather remaining stitches to close.

TAIL
Ch8 and sl st to join into a circle
Rnds 1-3 dc (3 rnds)
Rnd 4 dc6, dc2tog (7)
Rnd 5 dc5, dc2tog (6)
Rnd 6 dc4, dc2tog (5)
Rnd 7 dc3, dc2tog (4)
Do not stuff. Gather remaining stitches to close.

Finish by sewing eyes into place with Black yarn and nose with Cocoa yarn.

LEVEL 1 MILO THE DOG

GEORGINA
the Hippo

Georgina is a princess among hippos. Despite her PhD in something very scientific with a title that has an acronym longer than her name, her brain feels most tested when she is trying out the latest nail-art techniques on a Friday night. An evening in with takeaway sushi and reality TV is her perfect antidote to a stressful week in the office. She is fiercely loyal, a friend to everyone, and with never a whine, moan or grumble she is by far one of the most positive animals around the watering hole.

YARN REQUIRED

75g TOFT DK yarn Mushroom

See also: *You Will Need* and *Size Options*.

LEGS (make four)

Begin by dc6 into ring

Rnd 1 (dc2 into next st) 6 times (12)

Rnd 2 (dc1, dc2 into next st) 6 times (18)

Rnd 3 (dc2, dc2 into next st) 6 times (24)

Rnds 4-6 dc (3 rnds)

Rnd 7 (dc1, dc2tog) 8 times (16)

Rnd 8 (dc2, dc2tog) 4 times (12)

Rnds 9-24 dc (16 rnds)

Stuff the ends only and then fold flat and sew or dc through both sides of rnd across the top to close.

BODY

Work as STANDARD in Mushroom

HEAD

Begin by dc6 into ring

Rnd 1 (dc2 into next st) 6 times (12)

Rnd 2 (dc1, dc2 into next st) 6 times (18)

Rnd 3 (dc2, dc2 into next st) 6 times (24)

Rnds 4-8 dc (5 rnds)

Rnd 9 (dc2, dc2tog) 6 times (18)

Rnd 10 (dc1, dc2 into next st) 9 times (27)

Rnd 11 dc

Rnd 12 (dc8, dc2 into next st) 3 times (30)

Rnd 13 (dc9, dc2 into next st) 3 times (33)

Rnd 14 (dc10, dc2 into next st) 3 times (36)

Rnd 15 (dc11, dc2 into next st) 3 times (39)

Rnd 16 (dc12, dc2 into next st) 3 times (42)

Rnd 17 dc

Rnd 18 (dc1, dc2tog) 14 times (28)

Rnd 19 (dc5 dc2tog) 4 times (24)

Rnd 20 (dc2, dc2tog) 6 times (18)

Rnd 21 (dc2tog) 9 times (9)

Stuff and gather remaining stitches to close.

EARS (make two)

Begin by dc6 into ring

Rnd 1 (dc2 into next st) 6 times (12)

Rnds 2-5 dc (4 rnds)

Rnd 6 (dc2tog) 6 times (6)

Do not stuff. Gather remaining stitches to close.

TAIL

Create CHAIN TAIL: using four strands of yarn held together, ch8 sts with this oversized yarn then work three ch10 CHAIN LOOPS onto the end using a single strand (see *Technicals*)

NOSTRILS (make two)

Begin by dc6 into ring

Sew into position.

Finish by sewing eyes into place with Black yarn.

LEVEL 1 GEORGINA THE HIPPO

AUSTIN
the Rhino

Austin is a high-flying rhino. A private airline pilot with four daughters and a glamorous wife to keep in Jimmy Choos, he is a proud and hard-working father. When he's not in the captain's chair he's on the rowing machine in the gym or stretching his legs at breakneck speeds around the local park. He and his wife are often seen at the most high-falutin' cocktail bars in the world, easily recognised by their immaculately dyed hair, raucous laughter and the light glinting off their French-polished horns.

YARN REQUIRED

75g TOFT DK yarn Stone

See also: *You Will Need* and *Size Options*.

LEGS (make four)
Begin by dc6 into ring
Rnd 1 (dc2 into next st) 6 times (12)
Rnd 2 (dc1, dc2 into next st) 6 times (18)
Rnd 3 (dc2, dc2 into next st) 6 times (24)
Rnds 4-6 dc (3 rnds)
Rnd 7 (dc1, dc2tog) 8 times (16)
Rnd 8 (dc2, dc2tog) 4 times (12)
Rnds 9-24 dc (16 rnds)
Stuff the ends only and then fold flat and sew or dc through both sides of rnd across the top to close.

BODY
Work as STANDARD in Stone

HEAD
Begin by dc6 into ring
Rnd 1 (dc2 into next st) 6 times (12)
Rnd 2 (dc1, dc2 into next st) 6 times (18)
Rnd 3 (dc2, dc2 into next st) 6 times (24)
Rnd 4 (dc3, dc2 into next st) 6 times (30)
Rnd 5 (dc4, dc2 into next st) 6 times (36)
Rnd 6 (dc5, dc2 into next st) 6 times (42)
Rnds 7-11 dc (5 rnds)
Rnd 12 (dc5, dc2tog) 6 times (36)
Rnd 13 (dc4, dc2tog) 6 times (30)
Rnd 14 (dc3, dc2tog) 6 times (24)
Rnd 15 dc12, (dc1, dc2tog) 4 times (20)
Rnds 16-18 dc (3 rnds)
Rnd 19 (dc3, dc2 into next st) 5 times (25)
Rnds 20-22 dc (3 rnds)
Rnd 23 (dc3, dc2tog) 5 times (20)
Rnd 24 (dc2, dc2tog) 5 times (15)
Rnd 25 (dc1, dc2tog) 5 times (10)
Rnd 26 (dc2tog) 5 times (5)
Stuff and gather remaining stitches to close.

EARS (make two)
Begin by dc6 into ring
Rnd 1 (dc2 into next st) 6 times (12)
Rnds 2-5 dc (4 rnds)
Rnd 6 (dc2tog) 6 times (6)
Do not stuff. Gather remaining stitches to close.

HORN
Ch12 and sl st to join into a circle
Rnd 1 dc
Rnd 2 dc10, dc2tog (11)
Rnd 3 dc9, dc2tog (10)
Rnd 4 dc8, dc2tog (9)
Rnd 5 dc7, dc2tog (8)
Rnd 6 dc6, dc2tog (7)
Rnd 7 dc5, dc2tog (6)
Rnd 8 dc4, dc2tog (5)
Rnd 9 dc3, dc2tog (4)
Rnd 10 dc2, dc2tog (3)
Rnd 11 dc3tog (1)
Stuff and back stitch to sew into position.

TAIL
Sl st into position and ch9, turn and dc back down chain

Finish by sewing eyes into place with Black yarn.

LEVEL 1 AUSTIN THE RHINO

33

KARL
the Wallaby

Karl is a nanny with an absolute passion for every element of his job. Behind the starched grey uniform he has to wear, there's a fun-loving marsupial with a silly side saved especially for getting smiles through snotty tears. Packed-lunches made by this wallaby are always a work of art – him having mastered carving cucumbers, carrots and even cheese into tiny sculptures of every kind. Don't ever expect a jam sandwich and packet of crisps when you lift the lid – you're more likely to see Goldilocks and the three bears staring back at you.

YARN REQUIRED

75g TOFT DK yarn Shale

See also: *You Will Need* and *Size Options*.

LEGS (make four)
Work as STANDARD in Shale

BODY
Work as STANDARD in Shale

HEAD
Begin by dc6 into ring
Rnd 1 (dc2 into next st) 6 times (12)
Rnd 2 (dc1, dc2 into next st) 6 times (18)
Rnd 3 (dc2, dc2 into next st) 6 times (24)
Rnd 4 (dc3, dc2 into next st) 6 times (30)
Rnd 5 (dc4, dc2 into next st) 6 times (36)
Rnd 6 (dc5, dc2 into next st) 6 times (42)
Rnds 7-11 dc (5 rnds)
Rnd 12 (dc5, dc2tog) 6 times (36)
Rnd 13 (dc1, dc2tog) 6 times, dc18 (30)
Rnd 14 (dc3, dc2tog) 6 times (24)
Rnd 15 (dc2, dc2tog) 6 times (18)
Rnd 16 (dc1, dc2tog) 6 times (12)
Rnd 17 (dc1, dc2 into next st) 6 times (18)
Rnds 18-19 dc (2 rnds)
Rnd 20 (dc1, dc2tog) 6 times (12)
Rnd 21 (dc2tog) 6 times (6)
Stuff and gather remaining stitches to close.

EARS (make two)
Begin by dc6 into ring
Rnd 1 dc
Rnd 2 (dc2 into next st) 6 times (12)
Rnd 3 (dc1, dc2 into next st) 6 times (18)
Rnd 4 (dc2, dc2 into next st) 6 times (24)
Rnds 5-6 dc (2 rnds)
Rnd 7 (dc2, dc2tog) 6 times (18)
Rnd 8 (dc1, dc2tog) 6 times (12)
Rnd 9 (dc2, dc2tog) 3 times (9)
Do not stuff. Gather remaining stitches to close.

TAIL
Begin by dc6 into ring
Rnds 1-2 dc (2 rnds)
Rnd 3 dc2 into next st, dc5 (7)
Rnd 4 dc
Rnd 5 dc2 into next st, dc6 (8)
Rnds 6-7 dc (2 rnds)
Rnd 8 dc2 into next st, dc7 (9)
Rnds 9-10 dc (2 rnds)
Rnd 11 dc2 into next st, dc8 (10)
Rnds 12-13 dc (2 rnds)
Rnd 14 dc2 into next st, dc9 (11)
Rnds 15-17 dc (3 rnds)
Rnd 18 dc2 into next st, dc10 (12)
Rnd 19 dc2 into next st, dc11 (13)
Rnd 20 dc2 into next st, dc12 (14)
Rnd 21 dc2 into next st, dc13 (15)
Rnd 22 (dc4, dc2 into next st) 3 times (18)
Stuff and back stitch to sew into position.

Finish by sewing eyes into place with Black yarn.

LEVEL 1 KARL THE WALLABY

SIMON
the Sheep

Simon is a meticulous bachelor with little in his life to worry about. Following a minor hiccup a few years back, he swapped his overstretched mortgage for a red sports car, downsized to somewhere with a plasma TV bigger than the bathroom, and learned to wakeboard. Life as a dentist has never been a bad one; it gives Simon plenty of time to keep on top of his appearance, including the opportunity to check out how well trimmed his eyebrows are in the reflection of his customers' highly polished teeth. The future looks bright for a sheep who now has no need to ever learn how to boil an egg.

YARN REQUIRED

75g TOFT DK yarn Cream

See also: *You Will Need* and *Size Options*.

LEGS (make four)
Work as STANDARD in Cream

BODY
Work as STANDARD in Cream

HEAD
Begin by dc6 into ring
Rnd 1 (dc2 into next st) 6 times (12)
Rnd 2 (dc1, dc2 into next st) 6 times (18)
Rnd 3 (dc2, dc2 into next st) 6 times (24)
Rnd 4 (dc3, dc2 into next st) 6 times (30)
Rnd 5 (dc4, dc2 into next st) 6 times (36)
Rnd 6 (dc5, dc2 into next st) 6 times (42)
Rnds 7-11 dc (5 rnds)
Rnd 12 (dc5, dc2tog) 6 times (36)
Rnds 13-14 dc (2 rnds)
Rnd 15 dc4, (dc2tog) 3 times, dc26 (33)
Rnd 16 dc3, (dc2tog) 3 times, dc24 (30)
Rnd 17 dc
Rnd 18 (dc3, dc2tog) 6 times (24)
Rnds 19-21 dc (3 rnds)
Rnd 22 (dc2, dc2tog) 6 times (18)
Rnd 23 dc
Rnd 24 (dc1, dc2tog) 6 times (12)
Rnd 25 (dc2tog) 6 times (6)
Stuff and gather remaining stitches to close.

EARS (make two)
Begin by dc6 into ring
Rnd 1 (dc2 into next st) 6 times (12)
Rnds 2-5 dc (4 rnds)
Rnd 6 (dc2tog) 6 times (6)
Do not stuff. Gather remaining stitches to close.

TAIL
Begin by dc6 into ring
Rnd 1 (dc2 into next st) 6 times (12)
Rnds 2-4 dc (3 rnds)
Rnd 5 (dc2tog) 6 times (6)
Rnd 6 dc
Do not stuff. Gather remaining stitches to close.

FLEECE
Work ch8 CHAIN LOOPS all over the body leaving the bottom of body plain to ensure balance when sitting (see *Technicals*)

Finish by sewing eyes into place with Black yarn.

LEVEL 1 SIMON THE SHEEP

RUFUS
the Lion

Rufus is a bad plumber. His blindness to this fact has landed him in several very wet scenarios. Some of his most spectacularly disastrous incidents have included falling through a ceiling while clinging for dear life onto a water tank; calling the fire brigade to assist with his own tail being caught in a sink; and causing a large electrical explosion while installing a dehumidifier in his own very small cellar. He is well-intentioned in his sales pitch, but was perhaps sleeping through at least half of his night classes and got very lucky in his final exam. Thankfully, he came to the trade late in life after abandoning a successful career in daytime sales television, so retirement is just around the corner.

YARN REQUIRED

75g TOFT DK yarn Camel
25g TOFT DK yarn Fudge

See also: *You Will Need* and *Size Options*.

LEGS (make four)
Work as STANDARD in Camel

BODY
Work as STANDARD in Camel

HEAD
Working in Camel
Begin by dc6 into ring
Rnd 1 (dc2 into next st) 6 times (12)
Rnd 2 (dc1, dc2 into next st) 6 times (18)
Rnd 3 (dc2, dc2 into next st) 6 times (24)
Rnd 4 (dc3, dc2 into next st) 6 times (30)
Rnd 5 (dc4, dc2 into next st) 6 times (36)
Rnd 6 (dc5, dc2 into next st) 6 times (42)
Rnds 7-11 dc (5 rnds)
Rnd 12 dc10, dc2tog, dc5, dc2tog, dc10, dc2tog, dc5, dc2tog, dc4 (38)
Rnd 13 dc14, dc2tog, dc6, dc2tog, dc14 (36)
Rnd 14 (dc4, dc2tog) 6 times (30)
Rnd 15 (dc3, dc2tog) 6 times (24)
Rnd 16 dc9, dc2tog, dc2, dc2tog, dc9 (22)
Rnd 17 dc7, dc2tog, dc2, dc2tog, dc9 (20)
Rnds 18-23 dc (6 rnds)
Rnd 24 (dc2tog) 10 times (10)
Rnd 25 (dc2tog) 5 times (5)
Stuff and gather remaining stitches to close.

EARS (make two)
Working in Camel
Begin by dc6 into ring
Rnd 1 (dc2 into next st) 6 times (12)
Rnd 2 (dc1, dc2 into next st) 6 times (18)
Rnds 3-5 dc (3 rnds)
Rnd 6 (dc1, dc2tog) 6 times (12)
Rnd 7 (dc2tog) 6 times (6)
Do not stuff. Gather remaining stitches to close.

TAIL
Working in Camel
Create CHAIN TAIL: using four strands of yarn held together, ch18 sts with this oversized yarn then work six ch10 CHAIN LOOPS onto the end using a single strand in Fudge (see *Technicals*)

MANE
Working in Fudge
Work ch10 CHAIN LOOPS all over the top and sides of the head with three ch15 loops under the chin (see *Technicals*)

Finish by sewing eyes and nose into place with Black yarn.

LEVEL 1 RUFUS THE LION

BENEDICT
the Chimpanzee

Show-off Benedict hasn't stopped raving since the early 1990s and is never happier than when throwing shapes in the centre of a circle. He has a cheesy grin and a fixed thousand-yard stare that is only broken in the frenzied 10 minutes in which he needs to purchase next year's Glastonbury ticket. His wardrobe principally consists of a wide selection of neon bobble hats and flip-flops, which he supplements with various sweaty band T-shirts that he picks up on his travels. That said, in his job as head gardener at a stately home, he has won awards for his topiary maze design (and the plants don't care what he wears).

YARN REQUIRED

75g TOFT DK yarn Cocoa
25g TOFT DK yarn Camel

See also: *You Will Need* and *Size Options*.

ARMS (make two)
Working in Cocoa
Begin by dc6 into ring
Rnd 1 (dc2 into next st) 6 times (12)
Rnd 2 (dc1, dc2 into next st) 6 times (18)
Rnds 3-6 dc (4 rnds)
Rnd 7 (dc1, dc2tog) 6 times (12)
Rnds 8-30 dc (23 rnds)
Stuff end and sew flat across top to close.

LEGS (make two)
Work as STANDARD in Cocoa

BODY
Work as STANDARD in Cocoa

HEAD
Working in Cocoa
Begin by dc6 into ring
Rnd 1 (dc2 into next st) 6 times (12)
Rnd 2 (dc1, dc2 into next st) 6 times (18)
Rnd 3 (dc2, dc2 into next st) 6 times (24)
Rnd 4 (dc3, dc2 into next st) 6 times (30)
Rnd 5 (dc4, dc2 into next st) 6 times (36)
Rnd 6 (dc5, dc2 into next st) 6 times (42)
Rnds 7-11 dc (5 rnds)
Rnd 12 (dc5, dc2tog) 6 times (36)
Rnd 13 dc
Rnd 14 (dc4, dc2tog) 3 times, dc18 (33)
Rnd 15 (dc3, dc2tog) 3 times, dc18 (30)
Rnd 16 dc
Rnd 17 (dc3, dc2tog) 6 times (24)
Rnd 18 dc12, (dc1, dc2tog) 4 times (20)
Rnd 19 (dc2, dc2tog) 5 times (15)
Rnd 20 (dc2tog) 7 times, dc1 (8)
Stuff and gather remaining stitches to close.

EARS (make two)
Working in Camel
Begin by dc4 into ring
Rnd 1 (dc2 into next st) 4 times (8)
Rnd 2 (dc2 into next st) 8 times (16)
Rnds 3-4 dc (2 rnds)
Rnd 5 (dc2tog) 8 times (8)
Do not stuff. Pinch before sewing into position.

MUZZLE
Working in Camel
Begin by dc6 into ring
Rnd 1 (dc2 into next st) 6 times (12)
Rnd 2 (dc1, dc2 into next st) 6 times (18)
Rnd 3 (dc2, dc2 into next st) 6 times (24)
Rnds 4-7 dc (4 rnds)
Stuff and back stitch to sew into position.

EYE PATCHES (make two)
Working in Camel
Begin by dc6 into ring
Rnd 1 (dc2 into next st) 6 times (12)
Back stitch to sew into position.

Finish by sewing eyes and nostrils into place with Black yarn.

LEVEL 1 BENEDICT THE CHIMPANZEE

41

WINSTON
the Aardvark

Winston has four pet cats. He possesses a natural ability to make everyone smile with his ridiculously big grin that always quickly follows 'good morning', 'good afternoon' and 'good evening'. Other than tending to his pets and working towards his Grade 8 saxophone exam, he spends his spare time on the indoor ski slope. He hits the Alps three times a year clad in the same gear he's been wearing for far too many seasons. But if anyone's going to pull off a faded vintage onesie at 70 miles an hour, it's this innately cool aardvark.

YARN REQUIRED

50g TOFT DK yarn Mushroom
25g TOFT DK yarn Stone

See also: *You Will Need* and *Size Options*.

LEGS (make four)
Work as STANDARD in Mushroom

BODY
Work as STANDARD in Mushroom

HEAD
Working in Stone
Work as STANDARD BODY Rnds 1-6
Rnds 7-11 dc (5 rnds)
Rnd 12 (dc5, dc2tog) 6 times (36)
Rnd 13 (dc4, dc2tog) 6 times (30)
Rnd 14 dc
Rnd 15 (dc3, dc2tog) 6 times (24)
Rnd 16 dc
Rnd 17 (dc2, dc2tog) 6 times (18)
Rnds 18-24 dc (7 rnds)
Rnd 25 (dc1, dc2tog) 6 times (12)
Rnds 26-28 dc (3 rnds)
Rnd 29 (dc1, dc2 into next st) 6 times (18)
Do not gather sts.

Stuff the head and then rolling back the end of the nose dc a round of sts inside the snout two rows back from the end, then gather these sts to close.

EARS (make two)
Working in Stone
Ch10 and sl st to join into a circle
Rnds 1-4 dc (4 rnds)
Rnd 5 (dc4, dc2 into next st) twice (12)
Rnd 6 dc

Rnd 7 (dc5, dc2 into next st) twice (14)
Rnds 8-10 dc (3 rnds)
Rnd 11 (dc5, dc2tog) twice (12)
Rnd 12 (dc4, dc2tog) twice (10)
Rnd 13 (dc3, dc2tog) twice (8)
Rnd 14 (dc2, dc2tog) twice (6)
Rnd 15 dc
Rnd 16 (dc1, dc2tog) twice (4)
Do not stuff. Fold flat and sew or dc through both sides of rnd across the top to close.

TAIL
Working in Stone
Ch12 and sl st to join into a circle
Rnds 1-3 dc (3 rnds)
Rnd 4 dc2tog, dc10 (11)
Rnds 5-6 dc (2 rnds)
Rnd 7 dc2tog, dc9 (10)
Rnds 8-9 dc (2 rnds)
Rnd 10 dc2tog, dc8 (9)
Rnd 11 dc
Rnd 12 dc2tog, dc7 (8)
Rnd 13 dc
Rnd 14 dc2tog, dc6 (7)
Rnd 15 dc
Rnd 16 dc2tog, dc5 (6)
Rnd 17 dc
Gather tip stitches to close then stuff and backstitch into position.

Finish by sewing eyes into place with Black yarn.

LEVEL 1 WINSTON THE AARDVARK

43

GERMAINE
the Gorilla

Germaine is an OAG with attitude. She's everyone's surrogate grandma; she has a toy box full of wonders that she has collected over 60 years of babysitting and that has fired the imagination of hundreds of children. Her blue eyeshadow tells of an undying pride in her appearance and is so thick on her eyelids that many debate as to whether she ever washes it off. To keep herself in shape she marches over five miles a day looking through the neighbours' windows, always perfectly made-up, with her trousers tucked into her socks and a rain cap on.

YARN REQUIRED

75g TOFT DK yarn Steel
25g TOFT DK yarn Shale

See also: *You Will Need* and *Size Options*.

ARMS (make two)
Working in Steel
Begin by dc6 into ring
Rnd 1 (dc2 into next st) 6 times (12)
Rnd 2 (dc1, dc2 into next st) 6 times (18)
Rnds 3-6 dc (4 rnds)
Rnd 7 (dc1, dc2tog) 6 times (12)
Rnds 8-30 dc (23 rnds)

LEGS (make two)
Work as STANDARD in Steel

BODY
Work as STANDARD in Steel

HEAD
Working in Steel
Begin by dc6 into ring
Rnd 1 (dc2 into next st) 6 times (12)
Rnd 2 (dc1, dc2 into next st) 6 times (18)
Rnd 3 (dc2, dc2 into next st) 6 times (24)
Rnd 4 (dc3, dc2 into next st) 6 times (30)
Rnd 5 (dc4, dc2 into next st) 6 times (36)
Rnd 6 (dc5, dc2 into next st) 6 times (42)
Rnds 7-11 dc (5 rnds)
Rnd 12 (dc5, dc2tog) 6 times (36)
Rnd 13 dc
Rnd 14 (dc4, dc2tog) 3 times, dc18 (33)
Rnd 15 (dc3, dc2tog) 3 times, dc18 (30)
Rnd 16 dc
Rnd 17 (dc3, dc2tog) 6 times (24)
Rnd 18 dc12, (dc1, dc2tog) 4 times (20)
Rnd 19 (dc2, dc2tog) 5 times (15)
Rnd 20 (dc2tog) 7 times, dc1 (8)
Stuff and gather remaining stitches to close.

EARS (make two)
Working in Shale
Begin by dc6 into ring
Rnd 1 (dc2 into next st) 6 times (12)
Rnds 2-5 dc (4 rnds)
Do not stuff. Gather remaining stitches to close.

MUZZLE
Working in Shale
Begin by dc6 into ring
Rnd 1 (dc2 into next st) 6 times (12)
Rnd 2 (dc1, dc2 into next st) 6 times (18)
Rnd 3 (dc2, dc2 into next st) 6 times (24)
Rnds 4-6 dc (3 rnds)
Stuff and back stitch to sew into position.

EYE PATCH
Working in Shale
Ch16 and sl st to join into a circle
Rnd 1 (dc2 into next st) 4 times, dc4, (dc2 into next st) 4 times, dc4 (24)
Sew circle across starting chain to form a 'mask' shape with two rounded ends.

HAIR
Working in Steel
Work three ch10 CHAIN LOOPS onto top of head

Finish by sewing eyes and nostrils into place with Black yarn.

LEVEL 1 GERMAINE THE GORILLA

ISAAC
the American Bison

Issac is an independent handbag designer with a rich baritone voice that rattles your socks off when he sings. Successfully running his small business as a designer and maker, he's got life's balance just about right between paying the bills and keeping his blood pressure down. When he's not fiddling around with buckles and braces, sewing a bit of contrasting lining here and there, he's practising for his next performance with his Wednesday night choir. Complete with a magnificent appearance (enhanced by half a tub of beard oil and some patent leather brogues) he's ready to take the spotlight on the stage for his first solo performance.

YARN REQUIRED

50g TOFT DK yarn Chestnut
50g TOFT DK yarn Cocoa

See also: *You Will Need* and *Size Options*.

LEGS (make four)
Work as STANDARD in Chestnut

BODY
Work as STANDARD in Chestnut

HEAD
Working in Cocoa
Begin by dc6 into ring
Work as STANDARD BODY Rnds 1-6
Rnds 7-9 dc (3 rnds)
Rnd 10 (dc2, dc2 into next st) 6 times, dc24 (48)
Rnds 11-12 dc (2 rnds)
Rnd 13 (dc2, dc2tog) 12 times (36)
Rnd 14 dc
Rnd 15 (dc1, dc2tog) 6 times, dc18 (30)
Rnd 16 dc
Rnd 17 (dc2tog) 6 times, (dc2, dc2 into next st) 6 times (30)
Rnd 18 (dc2tog) 3 times, dc24 (27)
Rnd 19 (dc2tog, dc7) 3 times (24)
Rnd 20 (dc2tog, dc2) 6 times (18)
Rnd 21 (dc2tog, dc4) 3 times (15)
Rnd 22 (dc2tog, dc3) 3 times (12)
Rnd 23 (dc2tog, dc2) 3 times (9)
Stuff and gather remaining stitches to close.

EARS (make two)
Working in Cocoa
Begin by dc6 into ring
Rnd 1 (dc1, dc2 into next st) 3 times (9)
Rnd 2 dc
Rnd 3 (dc2, dc2 into next st) 3 times (12)
Rnds 4-6 dc (3 rnds)
Rnd 7 (dc2, dc2tog) 3 times (9)
Do not stuff. Gather remaining stitches to close.

HORNS (make two)
Working in Chestnut
Ch9 and sl st to join into a circle
Rnds 1-4 dc (4 rnds)
Rnd 5 dc2tog, dc7 (8)
Rnd 6 dc2tog, dc6 (7)
Rnd 7 dc2tog, dc5 (6)
Rnd 8 dc2tog, dc4 (5)
Rnd 9 dc
Rnd 10 dc2tog, dc3 (4)
Stuff and back stitch to sew into position.

MANE
Working in Cocoa
Work four rounds of ch8 CHAIN LOOPS all the way around head and under chin (leave back of head plain).
Work two rows of ch10 loops on top of head between horns.
Work ch15 loops under the chin

Working in Chestnut
Work approx. four rows of ch12 CHAIN LOOPS between shoulders working down the back with ch8 loops along the bottom (see *Technicals*)

TAIL
Working in Chestnut
Create CHAIN TAIL: using four strands of yarn held together, ch8 sts with this oversized yarn then work three ch12 CHAIN LOOPS onto the end using a single strand in Cocoa (see *Technicals*)

Finish by sewing eyes and nostrils into place with Black yarn.

LEVEL 1 ISAAC THE AMERICAN BISON

LEVEL 2

Level 2 animals introduce easy colour changing from one shade to another. Cut your yarn after the change if you have fully finished using the first colour in that piece leaving a short end. There's no need to sew or tie them in, simply leave them inside the piece. If you are moving back and forth between two colours such as creating stripes, then drop the colour not in use and pick it back up when you return to it. The floats will run on the inside of the piece.

PENELOPE the Bear

HANK the Dorset Down Sheep

FIONA the Panda

ANGHARAD the Donkey

DOUGLAS the Highland Cow

LAURENCE the Tiger

CHARDONNAY the Palomino Pony

ALICE the Zebra

AUDREY the Nanny Goat

BETH the Dutch Rabbit

ANDREW the Sea Otter

OWEN the Wildebeest

CLARENCE the Bat

FRANCIS the Hedgehog

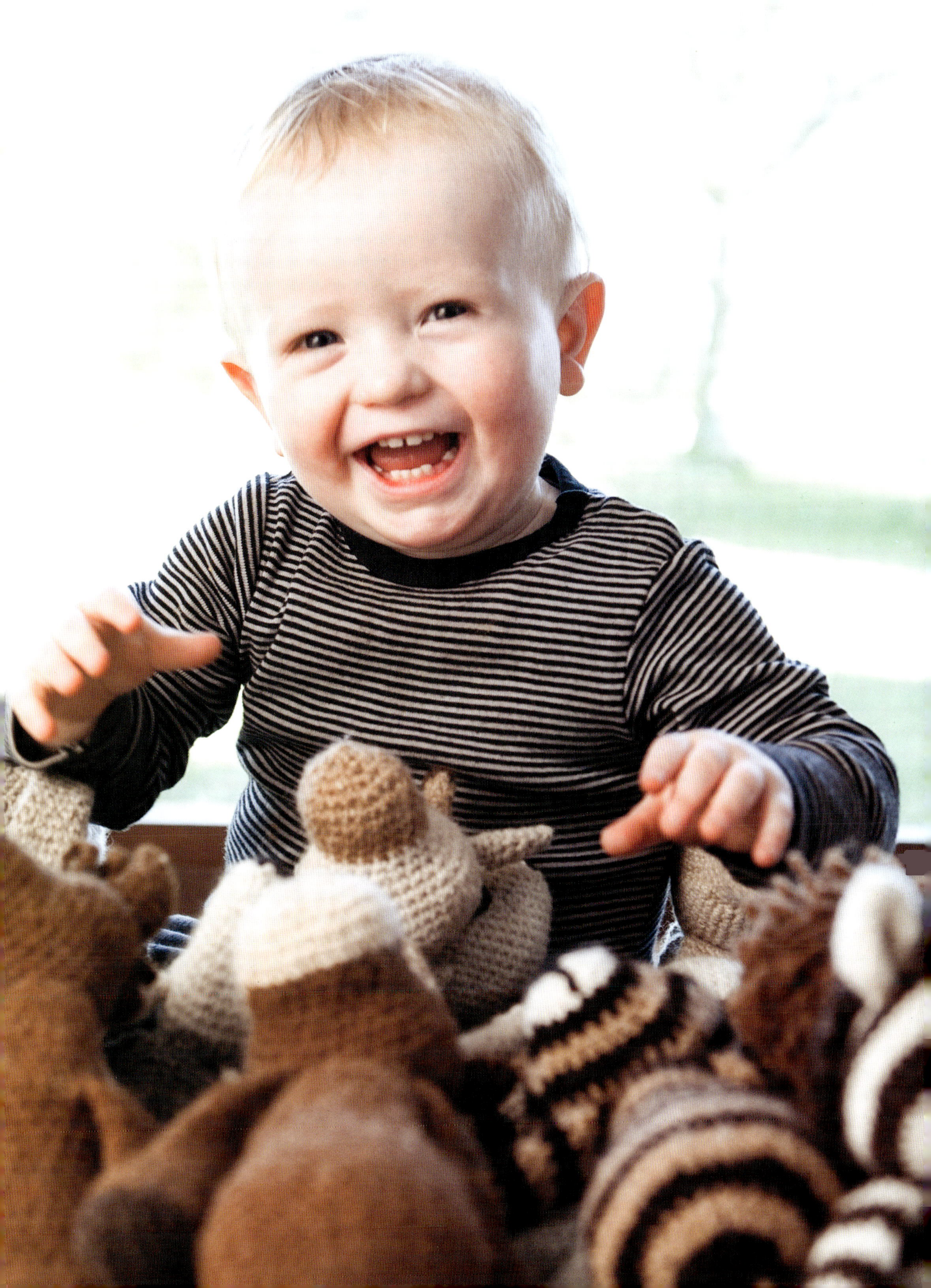

PENELOPE
the Bear

Penelope is a career bear at the top of her game. She expresses herself with her very extensive and obscenely expensive shoe collection. Possessing a very powerful blue-sky brain, she is a workaholic who gets results and brings out the best in any team she leads. Her signature drink is a complex champagne cocktail that no barman has ever heard of, but she is no party animal and has a reputation for always being the first to leave having secretly paid the whole bill. Her partner is equally impressive character, and together they will scuba dive the world.

YARN REQUIRED

50g TOFT DK yarn Fudge
25g TOFT DK yarn Oatmeal

See also: *You Will Need* and *Size Options*.

LEGS (make four)
Work as STANDARD in Fudge

BODY
Work as STANDARD in Fudge

HEAD
Working in Fudge
Begin by dc6 into ring
Rnd 1 (dc2 into next st) 6 times (12)
Rnd 2 (dc1, dc2 into next st) 6 times (18)
Rnd 3 (dc2, dc2 into next st) 6 times (24)
Rnd 4 (dc3, dc2 into next st) 6 times (30)
Rnd 5 (dc4, dc2 into next st) 6 times (36)
Rnd 6 (dc5, dc2 into next st) 6 times (42)
Rnds 7-11 dc (5 rnds)
Rnd 12 (dc5, dc2tog) 6 times (36)
Rnds 13-15 dc (3 rnds)
Rnd 16 dc10, (dc2, dc2tog) 4 times, dc10 (32)
Rnd 17 dc8, (dc2, dc2tog) 4 times, dc8 (28)
Change to Oatmeal
Rnd 18 dc6, (dc2, dc2tog) 4 times, dc6 (24)
Rnd 19 dc4, (dc2, dc2tog) 4 times, dc4 (20)
Rnd 20 dc4, (dc1, dc2tog) 4 times, dc4 (16)
Rnd 21 dc
Rnd 22 dc4, (dc2tog) 4 times, dc4 (12)
Rnd 23 (dc2tog) 6 times (6)
Stuff and gather remaining stitches to close.

EARS (make two)
Working in Fudge
Begin by dc6 into ring
Rnd 1 (dc2 into next st) 6 times (12)
Rnds 2-5 dc (4 rnds)
Rnd 6 (dc2tog) 6 times (6)
Do not stuff. Gather remaining stitches to close.

TAIL
Working in Fudge
Begin by dc6 into ring
Rnd 1 (dc2 into next st) 6 times (12)
Rnds 2-3 dc (2 rnds)
Rnd 4 (dc2tog) 6 times (6)
Rnd 5 (dc2tog) 3 times (3)
Do not stuff. Gather remaining stitches to close.

Finish by sewing eyes and nose into place with Black yarn.

LEVEL 2 PENELOPE THE BEAR

HANK
the Dorset Down Sheep

Hank is a seriously well-travelled ram with a ewe on every farm. Even as a newborn lamb he possessed a charm that melted all the midwives, and in his life he has continued to win the heart of every woman who crosses his path. He's a smooth-talking stud of a sheep who carries his 12-string guitar on his back wherever he goes. Every year his fleece gets hand-spun by his grandmother and knitted up into an intricate Aran jumper that keeps him warm through the unpredictable British summers.

YARN REQUIRED

50g TOFT DK yarn Cream
50g TOFT DK yarn Mushroom

See also: *You Will Need* and *Size Options*.

LEGS (make four)
Work as STANDARD in Mushroom

BODY
Work as STANDARD in Mushroom

HEAD
Working in Cream
Begin by dc6 into ring
Rnd 1 (dc2 into next st) 6 times (12)
Rnd 2 (dc1, dc2 into next st) 6 times (18)
Rnd 3 (dc2, dc2 into next st) 6 times (24)
Rnd 4 (dc3, dc2 into next st) 6 times (30)
Rnd 5 (dc4, dc2 into next st) 6 times (36)
Rnd 6 (dc5, dc2 into next st) 6 times (42)
Rnds 7-11 dc (5 rnds)
Rnd 12 (dc5, dc2tog) 6 times (36)
Rnds 13-14 dc (2 rnds)
Rnd 15 dc4, (dc2tog) 3 times, dc26 (33)
Rnd 16 dc3, (dc2tog) 3 times, dc24 (30)
Rnd 17 dc
Rnd 18 (dc3, dc2tog) 6 times (24)
Change to Mushroom
Rnds 19-21 dc (3 rnds)
Rnd 22 (dc2, dc2tog) 6 times (18)
Rnd 23 dc
Rnd 24 (dc1, dc2tog) 6 times (12)
Rnd 25 (dc2tog) 6 times (6)
Stuff and gather remaining stitches to close.

EARS (make two)
Working in Mushroom
Begin by dc6 into ring
Rnd 1 (dc2 into next st) 6 times (12)
Rnds 2-5 dc (4 rnds)
Rnd 6 (dc2tog) 6 times (6)
Do not stuff. Gather remaining stitches to close.

TAIL
Working in Mushroom
Begin by dc6 into ring
Rnd 1 (dc2 into next st) 6 times (12)
Rnds 2-4 dc (3 rnds)
Rnd 5 (dc2tog) 6 times (6)
Rnd 6 dc
Do not stuff. Gather remaining stitches to close.

FLEECE
Working in Cream, work ch8 CHAIN LOOPS all over the body and Cream section of head. Swap to ch4 loops at the bottom of the body to ensure balance when sitting (see *Technicals*)

LEVEL 2 HANK THE DORSET DOWN SHEEP

FIONA
the Panda

Fiona is a student. One thing this very brainy panda has never turned her mind to during her three years at university is the development of time-management skills good enough to keep her on top of her laundry pile. Only when her chest of drawers stands empty and she is clothed in someone else's borrowed pyjamas will she contemplate hauling a month's worth of clothes to the launderette for a full day of washing and drying. She applies a similar philosophy to her crockery, and is frequently caught microwaving noodles in her teapot before reaching for the washing-up liquid.

YARN REQUIRED

50g TOFT DK yarn Charcoal
50g TOFT DK yarn Cream

See also: *You Will Need* and *Size Options*.

LEGS (make four)
Working as STANDARD in Charcoal

BODY
Working as STANDARD in Cream changing to Charcoal after Rnd 17

HEAD
Working in Cream
Begin by dc6 into ring
Rnd 1 (dc2 into next st) 6 times (12)
Rnd 2 (dc1, dc2 into next st) 6 times (18)
Rnd 3 (dc2, dc2 into next st) 6 times (24)
Rnd 4 (dc3, dc2 into next st) 6 times (30)
Rnd 5 (dc4, dc2 into next st) 6 times (36)
Rnd 6 (dc5, dc2 into next st) 6 times (42)
Rnds 7-11 dc (5 rnds)
Rnd 12 (dc6, dc2 into next st) 6 times (48)
Rnds 13-14 dc (2 rnds)
Rnd 15 (dc2, dc2tog) 8 times, dc16 (40)
Rnd 16 (dc1, dc2tog) 8 times, dc16 (32)
Rnd 17 dc2, (dc2tog) twice, dc26 (30)
Rnd 18 (dc3, dc2tog) 6 times (24)
Rnd 19 (dc2, dc2tog) 6 times (18)
Rnds 20-22 dc (3 rnds)
Rnd 23 (dc2tog) 9 times (9)
Stuff and gather remaining stitches to close.

EARS (make two)
Working in Charcoal
Begin by dc6 into ring
Rnd 1 (dc2 into next st) 6 times (12)
Rnds 2-5 dc (4 rnds)
Rnd 6 (dc2tog) 6 times (6)
Do not stuff. Gather remaining stitches to close.

EYES (make two)
Working in Charcoal
Ch5 and work around chain as follows:
Rnd 1 dc3, dc2 into next st along one side of chain, dc3, dc2 into next st along other side of chain (10)

TAIL
Working in Cream
Begin by dc6 into ring
Rnd 1 (dc2 into next st) 6 times (12)
Rnds 2-3 dc (2 rnds)
Rnd 4 (dc2tog) 6 times (6)
Rnd 5 (dc2tog) 3 times (3)
Do not stuff. Gather remaining stitches to close.

Finish by sewing eyes and nose and mouth into place with Black yarn.

LEVEL 2 FIONA THE PANDA

ANGHARAD
the Donkey

Angharad is a surfer. In her VW camper she travels the south coast of the UK chasing waves in all seasons. A seaside donkey who never got over the feel of the sand and the taste of salt, she's enjoying her retirement in a wetsuit with no obligation to carry children around. She takes her cream tea with the jam first and is mortally offended if it's raspberry not strawberry. She is a collector of shells and unusual stones and can always be caught on the beach with her ass in the air happily minding her own business.

YARN REQUIRED

50g TOFT DK yarn Steel
25g TOFT DK yarn Cream

See also: *You Will Need* and *Size Options*.

LEGS (make four)
Work as STANDARD in Cream changing to Steel after Rnd 9

BODY
Work as STANDARD in Steel

HEAD
Working in Steel
Begin by dc6 into ring
Rnd 1 (dc2 into next st) 6 times (12)
Rnd 2 (dc1, dc2 into next st) 6 times (18)
Rnd 3 (dc2, dc2 into next st) 6 times (24)
Rnd 4 (dc3, dc2 into next st) 6 times (30)
Rnd 5 (dc4, dc2 into next st) 6 times (36)
Rnd 6 (dc5, dc2 into next st) 6 times (42)
Rnds 7-12 dc (6 rnds)
Rnd 13 (dc5, dc2tog) 6 times (36)
Rnd 14 (dc1, dc2tog) 12 times (24)
Rnd 15 (dc2, dc2tog) 6 times (18)
Change to Cream
Rnds 16-22 (7 rnds)
Rnd 23 (dc1, dc2tog) 6 times (12)
Rnd 24 (dc2tog) 6 times (6)
Stuff and gather remaining stitches to close.

EARS (make two)
Working in Steel
Ch20 and sl st to join into a circle
Rnd 1 (dc8, dc2tog) twice (18)
Rnd 2 dc
Rnd 3 (dc7, dc2tog) twice (16)
Rnds 4-7 dc (4 rnds)
Rnd 8 (dc6, dc2tog) twice (14)
Rnd 9 dc
Rnd 10 (dc5, dc2tog) twice (12)
Rnd 11 (dc2, dc2tog) 3 times (9)
Rnd 12 (dc1, dc2tog) 3 times (6)
Do not stuff. Fold flat and sew or dc through both sides of rnd to close.

TAIL
Working in Steel
Create CHAIN TAIL: using four strands of yarn held together, ch8 sts with this oversized yarn then work three ch15 CHAIN LOOPS onto the end using a single strand (see *Technicals*)

MANE
Working in Steel
Work ch12 CHAIN LOOPS on top of the head between the ears (see *Technicals*)

Finish by sewing eyes into place with Black yarn and nose with Steel yarn.

LEVEL 2 ANGHARAD THE DONKEY

DOUGLAS
the Highland Cow

Douglas is a family bull with a heart even bigger than his massive head. He has a tendency towards being very tidy and, when left alone, loves nothing more than dusting around the house in his brightly coloured pants. He has an insatiable appetite, but is quite a health-conscious soul who has made a habit of reading the nutritional information on all the food in the supermarket. Endlessly well intentioned, but occasionally blinded by hunger, he has been known (more than once) to land himself short of a sandwich and white-knuckle-grasping the wrong end of a stick.

YARN REQUIRED

75g TOFT DK yarn Fudge
25g TOFT DK yarn Oatmeal
25g TOFT DK yarn Charcoal

See also: *You Will Need* and *Size Options*.

LEGS (make four)
Work as STANDARD in Charcoal changing to Fudge after Rnd 5

BODY
Work as STANDARD in Fudge

HEAD
Working in Fudge
Work as STANDARD BODY Rnds 1-6
Rnds 7-11 dc (5 rnds)
Rnd 12 (dc5, dc2tog) 6 times (36)
Rnd 13 dc
Rnd 14 (dc4, dc2tog) 3 times, dc18 (33)
Rnd 15 (dc3, dc2tog) 3 times, dc18 (30)
Rnd 16 dc
Rnd 17 (dc3, dc2tog) 6 times (24)
Change to Oatmeal
Rnd 18 (dc3, dc2 into next st) 6 times (30)
Rnds 19-21 dc (3 rnds)
Rnd 22 (dc3, dc2tog) 6 times (24)
Rnd 23 (dc2, dc2tog) 6 times (18)
Rnd 24 (dc1, dc2tog) 6 times (12)
Stuff and gather remaining stitches to close.

EARS (make two)
Working in Fudge
Begin by dc6 into ring
Rnd 1 (dc2 into next st) 6 times (12)
Rnds 2-6 dc (5 rnds)
Rnd 7 (dc2tog) 6 times (6)
Do not stuff. Gather remaining stitches to close.

HORNS (make two)
Working in Oatmeal
Ch10 and sl st to join into a circle
Rnd 1 dc
Rnd 2 dc2tog, dc8 (9)
Rnd 3 dc
Rnd 4 dc2tog, dc7 (8)
Rnd 5 dc
Rnd 6 dc2tog, dc6 (7)
Rnd 7 dc
Rnd 8 dc2tog, dc5 (6)
Rnd 9 dc
Rnd 10 (dc2tog) 3 times (3)
Stuff and back stitch to sew into position.

TAIL
Working in Fudge
Create CHAIN TAIL: using four strands of yarn held together, ch6 sts with this oversized yarn then work three ch12 CHAIN LOOPS onto the end using a single strand (see *Technicals*)

TOPKNOT
Working in Fudge
Work ch10 CHAIN LOOPS on top of the head between the ears (see *Technicals*)

Finish by sewing eyes into place with Black yarn.

LEVEL 2 DOUGLAS THE HIGHLAND COW

LAURENCE
the Tiger

Laurence is a foodie who is utterly convinced that he is fluent in every language, but in reality speaks only a few quite badly. Chivalrous to the extreme, he has missed many a train by carrying bags up and down stairs for tigresses in distress, and is secretly shivering when socialising with female friends. Perhaps chivalry goes hand in hand with romance, for this tiger wines and dines in style. He'll happily spend all day making pasta, slow-roasting lamb and hand-rolling sushi, only to spend all night eating and whispering sweet nonsensical nothings to one very lucky lady.

YARN REQUIRED

50g TOFT DK yarn Camel
50g TOFT DK yarn Charcoal
25g TOFT DK yarn Cream

See also: *You Will Need* and *Size Options*.

STRIPE PATTERN

Starting in Camel work 2 rnds Camel, 2 rnds Charcoal

LEGS (make four)

Work as STANDARD in Charcoal changing to STRIPE PATTERN after Rnd 2

BODY

Work as STANDARD in Charcoal changing to STRIPE PATTERN after Rnd 1

HEAD

Working in Charcoal
Begin by dc6 into ring
Rnd 1 (dc2 into next st) 6 times (12)
Change to STRIPE PATTERN
Rnd 2 (dc1, dc2 into next st) 6 times (18)
Rnd 3 (dc2, dc2 into next st) 6 times (24)
Rnd 4 (dc3, dc2 into next st) 6 times (30)
Rnd 5 (dc4, dc2 into next st) 6 times (36)
Rnd 6 (dc5, dc2 into next st) 6 times (42)
Rnds 7-11 dc (5 rnds)
Rnd 12 dc10, dc2tog, (dc5, dc2tog) 3 times, dc9 (38)
Rnd 13 dc14, dc2tog, dc6, dc2tog, dc14 (36)
Rnd 14 (dc4, dc2tog) 6 times (30)
Rnd 15 (dc3, dc2tog) 6 times (24)
Rnd 16 dc9, dc2tog, dc2, dc2tog, dc9 (22)
Rnd 17 dc7, dc2tog, dc2, dc2tog, dc9 (20)
Continue in Cream
Rnds 18-19 dc (2 rnds)
Rnd 20 (dc2tog) 10 times (10)
Rnd 21 (dc2tog) 5 times (5)
Stuff and gather remaining stitches to close.

EARS (make two)

Working in Camel
Begin by dc6 into ring
Rnd 1 (dc2 into next st) 6 times (12)
Rnds 2-4 dc (3 rnds)
Change to Charcoal
Rnd 5 dc
Rnd 6 (dc2tog) 6 times (6)
Do not stuff. Gather remaining stitches to close.

TAIL

Working in Charcoal
Begin by dc6 into ring
Rnds 1-6 dc (6 rnds)
Change to STRIPE PATTERN
Rnds 7-26 dc (20 rnds)
Do not stuff.

Finish by sewing eyes and nose into place with Black yarn.

LEVEL 2 LAURENCE THE TIGER

CHARDONNAY
the Palomino Pony

Chardonnay is a glitter girl whose sharp business sense hides behind her white shoes and fake tan. As the owner of a luxury dog spa where rich and famous pooches come to get pampered, she is certainly used to being her own boss. It's all diamantés on toenails, sparkly suede collars and hand-knitted cashmere hoodies for these seriously indulged pets and the lady who makes it all happen. She has been online dating for the last two years and is tiring of someone else picking up the bill, especially as she's never yet found conversation to match the quality of the caviar.

YARN REQUIRED

75g TOFT DK yarn Camel
25g TOFT DK yarn Oatmeal

See also: *You Will Need* and *Size Options*.

LEGS (make four)
Work as STANDARD in Oatmeal changing to Camel after Rnd 8

BODY
Work as STANDARD in Camel

HEAD
Working in Camel
Begin by dc6 into ring
Rnd 1 (dc2 into next st) 6 times (12)
Rnd 2 (dc1, dc2 into next st) 6 times (18)
Rnd 3 (dc2, dc2 into next st) 6 times (24)
Rnd 4 (dc3, dc2 into next st) 6 times (30)
Rnd 5 (dc4, dc2 into next st) 6 times (36)
Rnd 6 (dc5, dc2 into next st) 6 times (42)
Rnds 7-12 dc (6 rnds)
Rnd 13 (dc5, dc2tog) 6 times (36)
Rnd 14 (dc1, dc2tog) 12 times (24)
Rnd 15 (dc2, dc2tog) 6 times (18)
Rnd 16 (dc2, dc2 into next st) 6 times (24)
Rnds 17-23 dc (7 rnds)
Rnd 24 (dc2, dc2tog) 6 times (18)
Rnd 25 (dc1, dc2tog) 6 times (12)
Stuff and gather remaining stitches to close.

EARS (make two)
Working in Camel
Begin by dc6 into ring
Rnd 1 (dc2 into next st) 6 times (12)
Rnd 2 (dc1, dc2 into next st) 6 times (18)
Rnds 3-4 dc (2 rnds)
Rnd 5 (dc1, dc2tog) 6 times (12)
Rnd 6 dc
Rnd 7 (dc2tog) 6 times (6)
Do not stuff. Gather remaining stitches to close.

MANE
Working in Oatmeal
Work ch12 CHAIN LOOPS up the back of the head and between the ears (see *Technicals*)

TAIL
Working in Oatmeal
Work six ch30 CHAIN LOOPS into tail position (see *Technicals*)

Finish by sewing eyes into place with Black yarn.

LEVEL 2 CHARDONNAY THE PALOMINO PONY

ALICE
the Zebra

Alice is one of those best kinds of friends. She leads a staunchly independent life working hard, and when she's not knee-deep designing logos she's chasing the party around the world with an overloaded suitcase that doesn't quite close. While she is distracted by taste-testing her way across the finest delis in London, or planning her annual mane trim, you'll never hear a word out of her. But with this zebra you need never worry if the phone doesn't ring; the moment your lives collide again it will be just like the last time you met.

YARN REQUIRED

50g TOFT DK yarn Charcoal
25g TOFT DK yarn Cream

See also: *You Will Need* and *Size Options*.

STRIPE PATTERN

Work 2 rounds Charcoal, 2 rounds Cream starting in colour stated

LEGS (make four)

Work as STANDARD in Charcoal Rnds 1-10 then change to Cream and work STRIPE PATTERN to end

BODY

Work as STANDARD in STRIPE PATTERN starting in Charcoal

HEAD

Working in Cream
Begin by dc6 into ring
Rnd 1 (dc2 into next st) 6 times (12)
Change to STRIPE PATTERN starting in Charcoal
Rnd 2 (dc1, dc2 into next st) 6 times (18)
Rnd 3 (dc2, dc2 into next st) 6 times (24)
Rnd 4 (dc3, dc2 into next st) 6 times (30)
Rnd 5 (dc4, dc2 into next st) 6 times (36)
Rnd 6 (dc5, dc2 into next st) 6 times (42)
Rnds 7-12 dc (6 rnds)
Rnd 13 (dc5, dc2tog) 6 times (36)
Rnd 14 (dc1, dc2tog) 12 times (24)
Rnd 15 (dc2, dc2tog) 6 times (18)
Rnd 16 (dc2, dc2 into next st) 6 times (24)
Rnds 17 dc
Continue in Charcoal
Rnds 18-23 dc (6 rnds)
Rnd 24 (dc2, dc2tog) 6 times (18)
Rnd 25 (dc1, dc2tog) 6 times (12)
Stuff and gather remaining stitches to close.

EARS (make two)

Working in Cream
Begin by dc6 into ring
Rnd 1 (dc2 into next st) 6 times (12)
Rnd 2 (dc1, dc2 into next st) 6 times (18)
Rnds 3-4 dc (2 rnds)
Rnd 5 (dc1, dc2tog) 6 times (12)
Rnd 6 dc
Rnd 7 (dc2tog) 6 times (6)
Rnd 8 (dc2tog) 3 times (3)
Do not stuff. Gather remaining stitches to close.

TAIL

Working in Cream
Create CHAIN TAIL: using four strands of yarn held together, ch8 sts with this oversized yarn then work three ch15 CHAIN LOOPS onto the end using a single strand of Charcoal (see *Technicals*)

MANE

Working in Charcoal
Work ch12 CHAIN LOOPS up the back of the head and between the ears to create a mane (see *Technicals*)

Finish by sewing eyes into place with Black yarn.

64

LEVEL 2 ALICE THE ZEBRA

AUDREY
the Nanny Goat

Audrey is a sharp-witted old goat with a penchant for sarcasm. She is a bit of a prankster and will take a schoolboy trick further than any eleven-year-old kid would dare. She takes all her hot drinks black and bitter, and saves up her annual dairy quota to be redeemed in one big cream liqueur binge in the days surrounding Christmas. Children have always found her a bit scary, as it's impossible to judge whether she's being serious or whether she's just got hold of your leg and is dragging you down the river towards a tasty-looking piece of foliage.

YARN REQUIRED

50g TOFT DK yarn Shale
25g TOFT DK yarn Cream

See also: *You Will Need* and *Size Options*.

LEGS (make four)
Work as STANDARD starting in Cream changing to Shale after Rnd 14

BODY
Work as STANDARD in Shale

HEAD
Working in Shale
Begin by dc6 into ring
Rnd 1 (dc2 into next st) 6 times (12)
Rnd 2 (dc1, dc2 into next st) 6 times (18)
Rnd 3 (dc2, dc2 into next st) 6 times (24)
Rnd 4 (dc3, dc2 into next st) 6 times (30)
Rnd 5 (dc4, dc2 into next st) 6 times (36)
Rnd 6 (dc5, dc2 into next st) 6 times (42)
Rnds 7-12 dc (6 rnds)
Rnd 13 (dc5, dc2tog) 6 times (36)
Rnd 14 (dc1, dc2tog) 12 times (24)
Rnd 15 dc6, (dc1, dc2tog) 6 times (18)
Rnds 16-18 dc (3 rnds)
Change to Cream
Rnds 19-21 dc (3 rnds)
Rnd 22 (dc2tog) 9 times (9)
Stuff and gather remaining stitches to close.

EARS (make two)
Working in Shale
Ch10 and sl st to join into a circle
Rnds 1-4 dc (4 rnds)
Rnd 5 (dc4, dc2 into next st) twice (12)
Rnd 6 dc
Rnd 7 (dc5, dc2 into next st) twice (14)
Rnds 8-10 dc (3 rnds)
Rnd 11 (dc5, dc2tog) twice (12)
Rnd 12 (dc4, dc2tog) twice (10)
Rnd 13 (dc3, dc2tog) twice (8)
Rnd 14 (dc2, dc2tog) twice (6)
Rnd 15 dc
Do not stuff. Gather tip, fold flat and sew or dc through both sides of rnd to close.

HORNS (make two)
Working in Cream
Ch8 and sl st to join into a circle
Rnds 1-4 dc (4 rnds)
Rnd 5 (dc2, dc2tog) twice (6)
Rnd 6 dc
Rnd 7 (dc2tog) 3 times (3)
Stuff and back stitch to sew into position.

TAIL
Working in Shale
Create CHAIN TAIL: using four strands of yarn held together, ch8 sts with this oversized yarn then work three ch8 CHAIN LOOPS onto the end using a single strand (see *Technicals*)

BEARD
Working in Cream
Work three ch12 CHAIN LOOPS into same st beneath chin (see *Technicals*)

Finish by sewing eyes and nose into place with Black yarn.

LEVEL 2 AUDREY THE NANNY GOAT

BETH
the Dutch Rabbit

Beth is a very kind, very wise and very, very tall rabbit. Equipped with her socks and sandals, you may have spotted her as a black and white flash striding past you in the supermarket in a direct line to the olives and hummus. A massive fan of every kind of vegetable, perhaps it's the consumption of all those greens that's the secret to her superpowers. Calm, collected and creative even in the face of chaos, this is the kind of rabbit you want to have on your team – no matter what the world throws at you!

YARN REQUIRED

50g TOFT DK yarn Charcoal
50g TOFT DK yarn Cream

See also: *You Will Need* and *Size Options*.

FRONT LEGS (make two)
Work as STANDARD in Cream

BACK LEGS (make two)
Work as STANDARD in Cream changing to Charcoal after Rnd 7

BODY
Work as STANDARD in Charcoal changing to Cream after Rnd 15

HEAD
Working in Charcoal
Begin by dc6 into ring
Rnd 1 (dc2 into next st) 6 times (12)
Rnd 2 (dc1, dc2 into next st) 6 times (18)
Rnd 3 (dc2, dc2 into next st) 6 times (24)
Rnd 4 (dc3, dc2 into next st) 6 times (30)
Rnd 5 (dc4, dc2 into next st) 6 times (36)
Rnd 6 (dc5, dc2 into next st) 6 times (42)
Rnds 7-11 dc (5 rnds)
Rnd 12 (dc5, dc2tog) 6 times (36)
Rnd 13 dc
Rnd 14 (dc2tog) 3 times, dc6, (dc2tog) 3 times, dc18 (30)
Rnds 15-16 dc (2 rnds)
Rnd 17 (dc4, dc2tog) 5 times (25)
Change to Cream
Rnd 18 dc
Rnd 19 (dc3, dc2tog) 5 times (20)
Rnd 20 (dc2, dc2tog) 5 times (15)
Rnd 21 (dc1, dc2tog) 5 times (10)
Stuff and gather remaining stitches to close.
Using Cream yarn sew a flash onto head above the colour change.

EARS (make two)
Working in Charcoal
Begin by dc6 into ring
Rnd 1 (dc1, dc2 into next st) 3 times (9)
Rnd 2 (dc2 into next st) 6 times, dc3 (15)
Rnds 3-15 dc (13 rnds)
Do not stuff. Fold flat and sew or dc through both sides of rnd across the top to close.

TAIL
Working in Charcoal
Begin by dc6 into ring
Rnd 1 (dc2 into next st) 6 times (12)
Rnds 2-4 dc (3 rnds)
Change to Cream
Rnd 5 (dc2tog, dc2) 3 times (9)
Rnd 6 (dc2tog, dc1) 3 times (6)
Rnd 7 (dc1, dc2tog) twice (4)
Do not stuff. Gather remaining stitches to close.

Finish by sewing eyes and nose into place with Black yarn.

LEVEL 2 BETH THE DUTCH RABBIT

69

ANDREW
the Sea Otter

Andrew is a sailor on a mission to map the seven seas and sample all 35 types of oyster on the way. At least, he currently believes that there are thirty-five types of oysters... although it seems that whenever he's completed his latest oyster map of the world, then he travels to a new place and someone adds another one on. Atlantic, Pacific, Belons and Kumamotos he loves them all and makes a point of trying each one raw always with a policy of chew, chew, and chew once more.

YARN REQUIRED

75g TOFT DK yarn Cocoa
25g TOFT DK yarn Oatmeal

See also: *You Will Need* and *Size Options*.

LEGS (make four)
Work as STANDARD in Cocoa

BODY
Work as STANDARD in Cocoa

HEAD
Working in Cocoa
Work as STANDARD BODY Rnds 1-6
Rnds 7-8 dc (2 rnds)
Change to Oatmeal
Rnds 9-10 dc (2 rnds)
Rnd 11 dc26, dc2tog, (dc4, dc2tog) twice, dc2 (39)
Rnd 12 dc26, dc2tog, (dc3, dc2tog) twice, dc1 (36)
Rnd 13 (dc4, dc2tog) 6 times (30)
Rnd 14 (dc3, dc2tog) 6 times (24)
Rnd 15 dc1, dc2tog, dc12, (dc1, dc2tog) 3 times (20)
Rnd 16 dc
Rnd 17 dc2, (dc1, dc2 into next st) 3 times, dc2, (dc2 into next st, dc1) 3 times, dc4 (26)
Rnd 18 dc
Rnd 19 (dc2tog) 13 times (13)
Rnd 20 (dc2tog) 6 times, dc1 (7)
Stuff and gather remaining stitches to close.

EARS (make two)
Working in Cocoa
Begin by dc6 into ring
Rnd 1 (dc2 into next st) 6 times (12)
Rnds 2-3 dc (2 rnds)
Do not stuff. Gather remaining stitches to close.

TAIL
Working in Cocoa
Ch24 and sl st to join into a circle
Rnds 1-2 dc (2 rnds)
Rnd 3 dc2tog, dc22 (23)
Rnd 4 dc2tog, dc21 (22)
Rnd 5 dc2tog, dc20 (21)
Rnd 6 dc2tog, dc19 (20)
Rnd 7 dc2tog, dc18 (19)
Rnd 8 dc2tog, dc17 (18)
Rnd 9 dc2tog, dc16 (17)
Rnd 10 dc2tog, dc15 (16)
Rnds 11-13 dc (3 rnds)
Rnd 14 dc2tog, dc14 (15)
Rnd 15 dc2tog, dc13 (14)
Rnds 16-18 dc (3 rnds)
Rnd 19 dc2tog, dc12 (13)
Rnd 20 dc2tog, dc11 (12)
Rnd 21 dc2tog, dc10 (11)
Rnd 22 dc2tog, dc9 (10)
Rnd 23 dc2tog, dc8 (9)
Rnds 24-26 dc (3 rnds)
Rnd 27 dc2tog, dc7 (8)
Rnd 28 dc2tog, dc6 (7)
Rnd 29 dc2tog, dc5 (6)
Stuff and back stitch to sew into position.

Finish by sewing eyes into place with Black yarn and nose with Cocoa yarn.

LEVEL 2 ANDREW THE SEA OTTER

OWEN
the Wildebeest

Owen lives in his shed. If you want to have a conversation with him you have to hoof your way through the door hanging off its hinges before stepping over the lawnmover, hopping around the chainsaw and tip-toeing between the rakes, hoes and brooms. If you're lucky he'll offer you a perch atop a rusty old bucket, before handing you a cup of sweet tea in a questionably brown mug he was given by the building society when he first got a mortgage for the house that's at the other end of the garden.

YARN REQUIRED

75g TOFT DK yarn Cocoa
25g TOFT DK yarn Stone

See also: *You Will Need* and *Size Options*.

LEGS (make four)
Work as STANDARD in Cocoa

BODY
Work as Standard in Cocoa with following Rnds in Stone:
13, 17, 20, 22, 24, 26, 28, 29

HEAD
Working in Stone
Work as STANDARD BODY Rnds 1-6
Rnds 7-11 dc (5 rnds)
Rnd 12 (dc5, dc2tog) 6 times (36)
Change to Cocoa
Rnd 13 (dc4, dc2tog) 6 times (30)
Rnd 14 (dc1, dc2tog) 6 times, dc12 (24)
Rnd 15 dc
Rnd 16 (dc2tog) 6 times, (dc2, dc2 into next st) 4 times (22)
Rnd 17 dc
Rnd 18 (dc2tog) 3 times, (dc3, dc2 into next st) 4 times (23)
Rnd 19 (dc2tog) twice, dc3, dc2 into next st, (dc5, dc2 into next st) twice, dc3 (24)
Rnd 20 (dc2tog) 12 times (12)
Stuff and gather remaining stitches to close.

EARS (make two)
Working in Cocoa
Ch8 and sl st to join into a circle
Rnds 1-2 dc (2 rnds)
Rnd 3 (dc1, dc2 into next st) 4 times (12)
Rnd 4 dc
Rnd 5 (dc3, dc2 into next st) 3 times (15)
Rnds 6-9 dc (4 rnds)
Rnd 10 (dc1, dc2tog) 5 times (10)
Rnd 11 (dc2tog) 5 times (5)
Do not stuff. Gather remaining stitches to close.

HORNS (make two)
Working in Stone
Begin by dc6 into ring
Rnd 1 (dc2 into next st) 6 times (12)
Rnd 2 (dc1, dc2 into next st) 6 times (18)
Rnds 3-5 dc (3 rnds)
Rnd 6 (dc2tog) 6 times, dc6 (12)
Rnd 7 dc
Rnd 8 dc2tog, dc10 (11)
Rnd 9 dc
Rnd 10 dc2tog, dc9 (10)
Rnd 11 dc2tog, dc8 (9)
Rnds 12-14 dc (3 rnds)
Rnd 15 (dc2 into next st) twice, dc2, (dc2tog) twice, dc1 (9)
Rnd 16 dc5, dc2tog, dc2 (8)
Stuff lightly and continue
Rnd 17 dc2, dc2 into next st, dc1, (dc2tog) twice (7)
Rnd 18 dc1, dc2 into next st, dc1, (dc2tog) twice (6)
Rnd 19 dc
Rnd 20 dc2, (dc2tog) twice (4)
Gather remaining stitches to close.

TAIL
Working in Stone, work six ch30 CHAIN LOOPS around one stitch (see *Technicals*)

MANE
Working in Cocoa, work one row of ch16 CHAIN LOOPS up the back of the head (see *Technicals*)

BEARD
Working in Stone starting from top of head beneath horns work four CHAIN LOOPS down both sides of the head as follows:
ch24 loop, ch20 loop, ch16 loop, ch12 loop
Change to Cocoa and work two rows of ch8 CHAIN LOOPS under chin (see *Technicals*)

Finish by sewing eyes into place with Black yarn.

LEVEL 2 OWEN THE WILDEBEEST

CLARENCE
the Bat

Clarence spends most of his waking hours in a hard hat. As a structural engineer he thoroughly enjoys his job hanging around under bridges drinking milky tea and mocking the truck driver who did not know that his trailer was higher than the clearance. He is a collector of expensive Persian rugs, which he uses to make his inadequately heated house a bit more comfortable. You can see your breath in every room with the exception of the large and very ugly conservatory where Clarence sensitively nurses hundreds of plants. When Clarence is not taking them to the local railway museum, his young nephews love nothing more than playing with their favourite uncle's Venus flytraps.

YARN REQUIRED

75g TOFT DK yarn Mushroom
25g TOFT DK yarn Charcoal

See also: *You Will Need* and *Size Options*.

FRONT LEGS (make two)
Work as STANDARD in Mushroom Rnds 1-7 then
Rnd 8 (dc4, dc2tog) twice (10)
Rnds 9-33 dc (25 rnds)
Stuff end and sew flat across top to close.

BACK LEGS (make two)
Work as STANDARD in Mushroom

BODY
Work as STANDARD in Mushroom

HEAD
Working in Mushroom
Work as STANDARD BODY Rnds 1-6
Rnds 7-11 dc (5 rnds)
Rnd 12 (dc5, dc2tog) 6 times (36)
Rnd 13 dc
Rnd 14 (dc4, dc2tog) 3 times, dc18 (33)
Rnd 15 (dc3, dc2tog) 3 times, dc18 (30)
Rnd 16 dc
Rnd 17 (dc3, dc2tog) 6 times (24)
Rnd 18 dc12, (dc1, dc2tog) 4 times (20)
Rnd 19 (dc2, dc2tog) 5 times (15)
Rnd 20 (dc2tog) 7 times, dc1 (8)
Stuff and gather remaining stitches to close.

EARS (make two)
Working in Mushroom
Ch20 and sl st to join into a circle
Rnd 1 (dc8, dc2tog) twice (18)
Rnd 2 dc
Rnd 3 (dc7, dc2tog) twice (16)
Rnds 4-7 dc (4 rnds)
Rnd 8 (dc6, dc2tog) twice (14)
Rnd 9 dc
Rnd 10 (dc5, dc2tog) twice (12)
Rnd 11 (dc2, dc2tog) 3 times (9)
Rnd 12 (dc1, dc2tog) 3 times (6)
Rnd 13 dc
Rnd 14 (dc2tog) 3 times (3)
Do not stuff. Gather tip, fold flat and sew or dc through both sides of rnd to close.

WINGS (work twice)
Working in Charcoal
Once stuffed and sewn together sl st under 'armpit', ch3 and sl st into body
Row 1 turn, dc3 into space between ch and body, sl st into next st down arm
Row 2 turn, dc3, sl st into next st down body
Row 3 turn, dc2 into next st, dc2, miss 1 st and sl st into next st down arm (4)
Row 4 turn, dc2 into next st, dc3, sl st into next st down body (5)
Rows 5-21 continue working back and fourth in the same way, increasing 1 st at the beginning of each row (17 rows)
Row 22 turn, dc18
Row 23 turn, dc15
Row 24 turn, dc12
Row 25 turn, dc9
Row 26 turn, dc6

Finish by sewing eyes and nostrils into place with Black yarn.

LEVEL 2 CLARENCE THE BAT

FRANCIS
the Hedgehog

Francis is a petrolhead: be careful crossing the road in front of him because (as he will tell you at great length) the exhaust he fitted to his uncle's old hatchback upped the power on his wheels by 18 per cent. Nothing gets his spines tingling more than showing off his obscenely loud bass bins to his mates in the car park of the local fast-food joint. He has been dating the same young sow for five years now and thinks she might be the one to make him settle down and start developing a taste for olives, backgammon and sensibly early nights.

YARN REQUIRED

75g TOFT DK yarn Fudge
25g TOFT DK yarn Cocoa

See also: *You Will Need* and *Size Options*.

LEGS (make four)
Work as STANDARD in Fudge

BODY
Work as STANDARD in Fudge

HEAD
Working in Fudge
Begin by dc6 into ring
Rnd 1 (dc2 into next st) 6 times (12)
Rnd 2 (dc1, dc2 into next st) 6 times (18)
Rnd 3 (dc2, dc2 into next st) 6 times (24)
Rnd 4 (dc3, dc2 into next st) 6 times (30)
Rnd 5 (dc4, dc2 into next st) 6 times (36)
Rnd 6 (dc5, dc2 into next st) 6 times (42)
Rnds 7-12 dc (6 rnds)
Rnd 13 (dc5, dc2tog) 6 times (36)
Rnd 14 (dc4 dc2tog) 6 times (30)
Rnd 15 (dc1, dc2tog) 10 times (20)
Rnd 16 (dc2tog) 4 times, dc12 (16)
Rnds 17-19 dc (3 rnds)
Rnd 20 (dc2, dc2tog) 4 times (12)
Rnd 21 (dc2, dc2tog) 3 times (9)
Rnd 22 (dc2tog) 4 times, dc1 (5)
Stuff and gather remaining stitches to close.

EARS (make two)
Working in Fudge
Begin by dc6 into ring
Rnd 1 (dc2 into next st) 6 times (12)
Rnds 2-4 dc (3 rnds)
Rnd 5 (dc2tog) 6 times (6)
Do not stuff. Gather remaining stitches to close.

SPINES
Working in Cocoa, work ch5 SLIP STITCH CHAINS over the back of body and head with 2 SLIP STITCH TRAVERSE sts in between each spine (see *Technicals*)

Finish by sewing eyes and nose into place with Black yarn.

LEVEL 2 FRANCIS THE HEDGEHOG

LEVEL 3

Level 3 animals introduce some more complex techniques, so it is advisable to have made at least one Level 1 and one Level 2 animal before embarking on these. Many of these patterns require the use of more demanding colour changing: rather than cutting the yarn, you run it along the wrong side of the fabric, passing the colours back and forth, being careful not to pull the changes too tight to avoid puckering the fabric. There are two types of patterns for animals with distinctive markings that colour their bodies. The giraffe and cheetah have contrast coloured spots that you can choose to work at random on the shape, whereas the ocelot and African painted dog have very strict patterns stated stitch by stitch that most will find more challenging to follow.

Some of these patterns also include loop stitch; this involves only one extra step to the standard double crochet stitch, so don't be intimidated by its appearance. Finally there's Jane the Pangolin with unique techniques to create her scales and is the only time you'll need to use a treble in the whole book.

SAMUEL the Koala

WILLIAM the Sloth Bear

BRADLEE the Grey Squirrel

CASPAR the Peary Caribou

SARAH the Friesian Cow

CAITLIN the Giraffe

ESME the Fox

BLAKE the Orangutan

HAMLET the Cheetah

JESSIE the Raccoon

NOAH the Zwartbles Sheep

CHRISTOPHE the Wolf

NATASHA the Two-Toed Sloth

NOUSHA the Persian Cat

PERRY the Guinea Pig

CYBIL the Sugar Glider

NOEL the Chipmunk

GINA the Hyena

ANDREA the Ocelot

SAVANNA the African Painted Dog

JANE the Pangolin

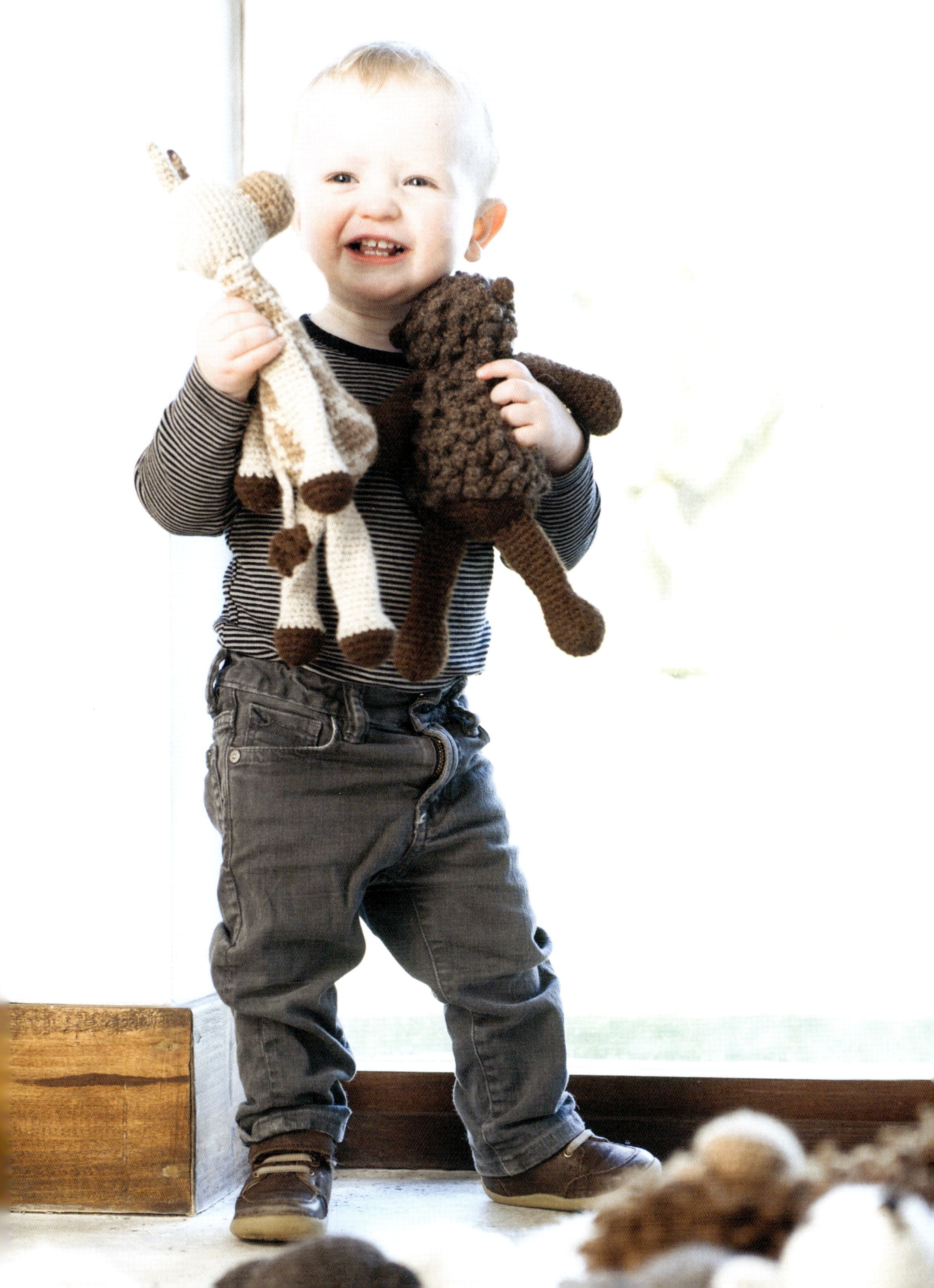

SAMUEL
the Koala

Samuel went on a gap year at the turn of the millennium and has never come back. In his travels around Europe he has become fluent in five languages and, as a current resident of Asia, has never tired of eating dim sum for breakfast. He has no place to call his own but instead keeps moving around; his home is wherever he takes his trainers off. He is a self-proclaimed artist who would maybe have something to show off, but he keeps losing track of his sketchbooks. Perhaps one day he will finally 'find himself' (and some drawings) in a bowl of pho soup and blow us all away with the talent he's been assuring us he has.

YARN REQUIRED

75g TOFT DK yarn Silver
25g TOFT DK yarn Charcoal

See also: *You Will Need* and *Size Options*.

LEGS (make four)
Work as STANDARD in Silver

BODY
Work as STANDARD in Silver

HEAD
Working in Silver
Begin by dc6 into ring
Rnd 1 (dc2 into next st) 6 times (12)
Rnd 2 (dc1, dc2 into next st) 6 times (18)
Rnd 3 (dc2, dc2 into next st) 6 times (24)
Rnd 4 (dc3, dc2 into next st) 6 times (30)
Rnd 5 (dc4, dc2 into next st) 6 times (36)
Rnd 6 (dc5, dc2 into next st) 6 times (42)
Rnd 7 (dc6, dc2 into next st) 6 times (48)
Rnds 8-12 dc (5 rnds)
Rnd 13 (dc4, dc2tog) 8 times (40)
Rnd 14 dc
Rnd 15 dc20, (dc1, dc2tog) 5 times, dc5 (35)
Rnd 16 dc20, (dc2tog) 5 times, dc5 (30)
Rnd 17 (dc3, dc2tog) 6 times (24)
Rnd 18 dc6, (dc1, dc2tog) 6 times (18)
Change to Charcoal
Rnds 19-21 dc (3 rnds)
Rnd 22 (dc2tog) 9 times (9)
Stuff and gather remaining stitches to close.

EARS (make two)
Working in Silver
Begin by dc6 into ring
Rnd 1 (dc2 into next st) 6 times (12)
Rnd 2 (dc1, dc2 into next st) 6 times (18)
Rnd 3 (dc2, dc2 into next st) 6 times (24)
Rnd 4 (dc3, dc2 into next st) 6 times (30)
Rnd 5 (dc4, dc2 into next st) 6 times (36)
Fold in half and dc with 1.5cm (½in) LOOP STITCH every st around the edge to close (see *Technicals*).

Finish by sewing eyes into place with Black yarn.

LEVEL 3 SAMUEL THE KOALA

81

WILLIAM
the Sloth Bear

Following a health scare in the early part of last year, William the sloth bear has been trying hard to take life a little more slowly. His recent enforced early retirement has taken him a bit of getting used to, and at his wife's behest he has been trying his best to start to enjoy spending a day standing waist deep in a freezing cold current. Despite having read every book in the library relating to trout and salmon behaviour, after a year of trying he still remains a decidedly poor fisherman, and is considering golf for the New Year.

YARN REQUIRED

75g TOFT DK yarn Charcoal
25g TOFT DK yarn Silver

See also: *You Will Need* and *Size Options*.

LEGS (make four)
Work as STANDARD in Charcoal

BODY
Work as STANDARD in Charcoal Rnds 1-21
Rnd 22 dc12 Charcoal, dc4 Silver, dc8 Charcoal (24)
Rnd 23 dc11 Charcoal, dc7 Silver, dc6 Charcoal
Rnds 24-26 dc10 Charcoal, dc2 Silver, dc4 Charcoal, dc2 Silver, dc6 Charcoal (3 rnds)
Rnd 27 (dc2, dc2tog) twice, dc2 Charcoal, dc2tog, dc1 Silver, dc1, dc2tog Charcoal, dc2 Silver, dc2tog, dc2, dc2tog Charcoal (18)
Continue in Charcoal
Rnd 28 dc
Rnd 29 (dc2tog) 9 times (9)

HEAD
Working in Charcoal
Begin by dc6 into ring
Rnd 1 (dc2 into next st) 6 times (12)
Rnd 2 (dc1, dc2 into next st) 6 times (18)
Rnd 3 (dc2, dc2 into next st) 6 times (24)
Rnd 4 (dc3, dc2 into next st) 6 times (30)
Rnd 5 (dc4, dc2 into next st) 6 times (36)
Rnd 6 (dc5, dc2 into next st) 6 times (42)
Rnds 7-11 dc (5 rnds)
Rnd 12 (dc5, dc2tog) 6 times (36)
Rnd 13 (dc1, dc2tog) 6 times, dc18 (30)
Rnd 14 (dc3, dc2tog) 6 times (24)
Rnd 15 (dc2, dc2tog) 6 times (18)

Change to Silver
Rnds 16-19 dc (4 rnds)
Rnd 20 (dc4, dc2tog) 3 times (15)
Rnd 21 (dc3, dc2tog) 3 times (12)
Rnd 22 (dc2, dc2tog) 3 times (9)
Stuff and gather remaining stitches to close.

EARS (make two)
Working in Charcoal
Begin by dc6 into ring
Rnd 1 (dc2 into next st) 6 times (12)
Rnd 2 (dc1, dc2 into next st) 6 times (18)
Work 2cm (¾in) LOOP STITCH every other st
Rnd 3 (dc2, dc2 into next st) 6 times (24)
Rnd 4 (dc3, dc2 into next st) 6 times (30)
Rnd 5 dc
Fold in half and dc with 2cm (¾in) LOOP STITCH every st around the edge to close.

TAIL
Working in Charcoal
Begin by dc6 into ring
Rnd 1 (dc2 into next st) 6 times (12)
Rnds 2-5 dc (4 rnds)
Rnd 6 (dc2tog) 6 times (6)
Rnd 7 (dc2tog) 3 times (3)
Do not stuff. Gather remaining stitches to close.

Finish by sewing eyes and nose into place with Black yarn.

LEVEL 3 WILLIAM THE SLOTH BEAR

83

BRADLEE
the Grey Squirrel

Bradlee is a sports squirrel. He can turn his rippling muscles to most field sports, but lacrosse silverware fills the majority of the shelves in his trophy cabinet. He's always been in with the in-crowd and works hard to keep his body and his reputation in peak condition. Each morning he does 30 push-ups and has a swim before breakfast. He closes each day with a weight-lifting session motivated by the trashy teenage angst music blaring out of his headphones. His heart is set on making waves in investment banking and everyone knows he's always the safe bet for a touchdown.

YARN REQUIRED

75g TOFT DK yarn Shale

See also: *You Will Need* and *Size Options*.

LEGS (make four)
Work as STANDARD in Shale

BODY
Work as STANDARD in Shale

HEAD
Begin by dc6 into ring
Rnd 1 (dc2 into next st) 6 times (12)
Rnd 2 (dc1, dc2 into next st) 6 times (18)
Rnd 3 (dc2, dc2 into next st) 6 times (24)
Rnd 4 (dc3, dc2 into next st) 6 times (30)
Rnd 5 (dc4, dc2 into next st) 6 times (36)
Rnd 6 (dc5, dc2 into next st) 6 times (42)
Rnds 7-11 dc (5 rnds)
Rnd 12 dc17, (dc2, dc2tog) 6 times, dc1 (36)
Rnd 13 dc
Rnd 14 (dc4, dc2tog) twice, (dc3, dc2tog) 4 times, dc4 (30)
Rnd 15 dc
Rnd 16 dc3, (dc2tog, dc3) 5 times, dc2tog (24)
Rnd 17 dc
Rnd 18 (dc2, dc2tog) 6 times (18)
Rnd 19 dc
Rnd 20 (dc2tog) 9 times (9)
Rnd 21 (dc2tog) 4 times, dc1 (5)
Stuff and gather remaining sts to close.

EARS (make two)
Begin by dc6 into ring
Rnd 1 (dc2 into next st) 6 times (12)
Rnds 2-5 dc (4 rnds)
Do not stuff.

TAIL
Ch15 and sl st to join into a circle
Work 3cm (1¼in) LOOP STITCH every other st
Rnds 1-28 dc (28 rnds)
Rnd 29 (dc2tog) 7 times, dc1 (8)
Stuff lightly, gather end, sew starting chain flat and sew into position securing up back with a few stitches.

Finish by sewing eyes and nose into place with Black yarn.

LEVEL 3 BRADLEE THE GREY SQUIRREL

CASPAR
the Peary Caribou

Around this time of year Caspar develops a bad habit of having one too many glasses of port at Christmas drinks get-togethers and begins evangelising about wood-burning stoves. He can bore anyone's festive socks off about the skills and care needed to chop the perfect sized log, and has become so obsessed by proving their efficiency that he's picked up a set of chimney brushes in the Black Friday sales, offering a free sweep to everyone he meets. It looks like he's set to be spending a lot of time up on the roof and guaranteed to sport a sooty beard this Christmas!

YARN REQUIRED

75g TOFT DK yarn Cream

See also: *You Will Need* and *Size Options*.

LEGS (make four)
Work as STANDARD in Cream

BODY
Work as STANDARD in Cream

HEAD
Work as STANDARD BODY Rnds 1-6

Rnds 7-11 dc (5 rnds)
Rnd 12 (dc5, dc2tog) 6 times (36)
Rnd 13 (dc4, dc2tog) 6 times (30)
Rnd 14 (dc3, dc2tog) 3 times, dc15 (27)
Rnd 15 (dc2, dc2tog) 3 times, dc15 (24)
Rnd 16 (dc1, dc2tog) 3 times, dc15 (21)
Rnd 17 dc

Work 2cm (¾in) LOOP STITCH as instructed

Rnds 18-19 dc10, (dc1 loop, dc1) 4 times, dc3 (2 rnds)
Rnd 20 dc6, dc2 into next st, dc5, dc1 loop, dc2 into next st, (dc1 loop, dc1) twice, dc2, dc2 into next st (24)

Continue without loops

Rnds 21-22 dc (2 rnds)
Rnd 23 (dc2tog) 12 times (12)
Rnd 24 (dc2, dc2tog) 3 times (9)

Stuff and gather remaining stitches to close.

EARS (make two)
Begin by dc6 into ring

Rnd 1 (dc2 into next st) 6 times (12)
Rnd 2 (dc1, dc2 into next st) 6 times (18)
Rnds 3-4 dc (2 rnds)
Rnd 5 (dc1, dc2tog) 6 times (12)
Rnd 6 dc
Rnd 7 (dc2tog) 6 times (6)
Rnd 8 (dc1, dc2tog) twice (4)

Do not stuff. Gather remaining stitches to close.

ANTLERS (make two)
Ch10 and sl st to join into a circle

Rnds 1-4 dc (4 rnds)
Rnd 5 (dc2 into next st) 4 times (incomplete rnd) (14)

Count 6 sts backwards and split these into a rnd of 6 sts and work as follows:

Rnds 1-4 dc (4 rnds)

Break yarn, rejoin and work remaining 8 sts as follows:

Rnd 1 dc6, dc2 into next st, dc1 (9)
Rnds 2-6 dc (5 rnds)
Rnd 7 (dc3 into next st) twice, dc2, dc3 into next st, dc4 (15)

Count 8 sts backwards and split these into a rnd of 8 sts and work as follows:

Rnds 1-5 dc (5 rnds)

Split into two rounds of 4 sts and work each as follows:

Rnd 1 dc3, dc2 into next (5)
Rnds 2-4 dc (3 rnds)

Break yarn, rejoin and work remaining 7 sts as follows:

Rnds 1-5 dc (5 rnds)

Count 4 sts backwards and split these into a rnd of 4 sts and work as follows:

Rnd 1 dc3, dc2 into next st (5)
Rnds 2-4 dc (3 rnds)

Break yarn, rejoin and work remaining 3 sts as follows:

Rnd 1 dc1, dc2 into next st, dc1 (4)
Rnd 2 dc2, dc2 into next st, dc1 (5)
Rnds 3-4 dc (2 rnds)

Stuff lightly, gather end stitches to close and sew into position.

TAIL
Begin by dc6 into ring

Rnd 1 (dc2 into next st) 6 times (12)
Rnds 2-5 dc (4 rnds)
Rnd 6 (dc2tog) 6 times (6)
Rnd 7 (dc2tog) 3 times (3)

Do not stuff. Gather remaining stitches to close.

Finish by sewing eyes into place with Black yarn.

LEVEL 3 CASPAR THE PEARY CARIBOU

SARAH
the Friesian Cow

Sarah works part-time in an ice-cream factory, stirring and whirling the finest locally sourced organic ingredients into the most mouth-watering pots of frozen yumminess. When she's not developing new recipes she is standing on the touchline cheering on any one of her four teenage boys, who all excel on the sports field. As a result she runs two toploading washing machines almost around the clock and knows exactly the correct temperature, soak time and spin cycle to select to guarantee perfect whites despite grass, mud and raspberry ripple.

YARN REQUIRED

50g TOFT DK yarn Charcoal
25g TOFT DK yarn Cream
25g TOFT DK yarn Oatmeal
Length of Cocoa for eyes

See also: *You Will Need* and *Size Options*.

LEGS (make four)

Work as STANDARD in Charcoal changing to Cream after Rnd 6

BODY

Work as STANDARD in Charcoal changing to Cream after Rnd 13 then back to Charcoal after Rnd 21

HEAD

Working in Charcoal

Begin by dc6 into ring

Rnd 1 (dc2 into next st) 6 times (12)
Rnd 2 (dc1, dc2 into next st) 6 times (18)
Rnd 3 (dc2, dc2 into next st) 6 times (24)
Rnd 4 (dc3, dc2 into next st) 6 times (30)
Rnd 5 (dc4, dc2 into next st) 6 times (36)
Rnd 6 (dc5, dc2 into next st) 6 times (42)
Rnds 7-11 dc (5 rnds)

Working LOOP STITCH when instructed

Rnd 12 dc7 with 2cm (¾in) loops in Cream, dc14 Charcoal, dc7 Cream, dc14 Charcoal
Rnd 13 dc7 with 2cm (¾in) loops in Cream, (dc2tog, dc5) twice Charcoal, dc7 Cream, (dc2tog, dc5) twice Charcoal (38)

Continue without loops

Rnd 14 dc2, (dc2tog) twice, dc2 Cream, dc11 Charcoal, dc8 Cream, dc11 Charcoal (36)
Rnd 15 dc6 Cream, (dc2tog) twice, dc7 Charcoal, dc9 Cream, dc6, (dc2tog) twice Charcoal (32)
Rnd 16 dc5 Cream, dc2tog, dc7 Charcoal, dc10 Cream, dc6, dc2tog Charcoal (30)
Rnd 17 dc1 Charcoal, dc1, dc2tog, dc1 Cream, (dc1, dc2tog) 3 times Charcoal, dc10 Cream, (dc1, dc2tog) twice Charcoal (24)

Continue in Cream

Rnds 18-19 dc (2 rnds)
Rnd 20 (dc2, dc2tog) 6 times (18)
Rnd 21 dc10 Cream, dc8 Oatmeal

Continue in Oatmeal

Rnd 22 (dc2, dc2 into next st) 6 times (24)
Rnd 23 (dc3, dc2 into next st) 6 times (30)
Rnd 24 dc
Rnd 25 (dc2tog) 15 times (15)
Rnd 26 (dc1, dc2tog) 5 times (10)

Stuff and gather remaining stitches to close.

EARS (make two)

Working in Charcoal

Begin by dc6 into ring

Rnd 1 (dc2 into next st) 6 times (12)
Rnds 2-6 dc (5 rnds)
Rnd 7 (dc2tog) 6 times (6)

Do not stuff. Gather remaining stitches to close.

TAIL

Working in Cream

Create CHAIN TAIL: using four strands of yarn held together, ch10 sts with this oversized yarn then work three ch12 CHAIN LOOPS onto the end using a single strand of Charcoal (see *Technicals*)

Finish by sewing eyes into place with Cocoa yarn.

LEVEL 3 SARAH THE FRIESIAN COW

89

CAITLIN
the Giraffe

Caitlin is one nosy giraffe. Life as a home science teacher just doesn't give her enough to talk about, but thankfully her active role as WI chairperson gives her the perfect excuse to know everyone else's business. That said, it's not as if she needs much gossip to go on; her skills at telling a tale mean she can spin richly elaborate scenarios from a tiny morsel of information. If you're ever wondering about the cousin of your neighbour's boyfriend's cat (or the shade of his pants), Caitlin is the one to ask.

YARN REQUIRED

75g TOFT DK yarn Oatmeal
25g TOFT DK yarn Camel

See also: *You Will Need* and *Size Options*.

LEGS (make four)

Work as STANDARD in Camel changing to Oatmeal after Rnd 6 then

Rnds 23-30 dc (8 rnds)

Sew front legs into position approx. 10 rnds from top of body.

BODY

Working in Oatmeal and working patches of Camel comprised of approximately 9 sts clustered over 3 or 4 rnds at random positions throughout

Begin by dc6 into ring

Rnd 1 (dc2 into next st) 6 times (12)
Rnd 2 (dc1, dc2 into next st) 6 times (18)
Rnd 3 (dc2, dc2 into next st) 6 times (24)
Rnd 4 (dc3, dc2 into next st) 6 times (30)
Rnd 5 (dc4, dc2 into next st) 6 times (36)
Rnd 6 (dc5, dc2 into next st) 6 times (42)
Rnd 7 (dc6, dc2 into next st) 6 times (48)
Rnds 8-12 dc (5 rnds)
Rnd 13 dc13, (dc4, dc2tog) 3 times, dc17 (45)
Rnd 14 dc
Rnd 15 (dc1, dc2tog) 15 times (30)
Rnds 16-20 dc (5 rnds)
Rnd 21 (dc3, dc2tog) 6 times (24)
Rnds 22-29 dc (8 rnds)
Rnd 30 (dc2, dc2tog) 6 times (18)
Rnds 31-33 dc (3 rnds)
Rnd 34 (dc1, dc2tog) 6 times (12)
Rnds 35-37 dc (3 rnds)
Rnd 38 (dc2tog) 6 times (6)

Stuff and gather remaining stitches to close.

HEAD

Working in Oatmeal

Work as STANDARD BODY Rnds 1-6

Rnds 7-11 dc (5 rnds)
Rnd 12 (dc5, dc2tog) 6 times (36)
Rnd 13 (dc4, dc2tog) 6 times (30)
Rnd 14 (dc3, dc2tog) 6 times (24)

Change to Camel

Rnd 15 dc12, (dc1, dc2tog) 4 times (20)
Rnds 16-19 dc (4 rnds)
Rnd 20 (dc2, dc2tog) 5 times (15)
Rnd 21 (dc1, dc2tog) 5 times (10)
Rnd 22 (dc2tog) 5 times (5)

Stuff and gather remaining stitches to close.

EARS (make two)

Working in Oatmeal

Ch9 and sl st to join into a circle

Rnds 1-5 dc (5 rnds)
Rnd 6 (dc1, dc2tog) 3 times (6)
Rnd 7 (dc2tog) 3 times (3)

Do not stuff. Gather remaining stitches to close.

TAIL

Working in Oatmeal

Create CHAIN TAIL: using four strands of yarn held together, ch6 sts with this oversized yarn then work three ch12 CHAIN LOOPS onto the end using a single strand of Camel (see *Technicals*)

OSSICONES (make two)

Working in Camel

Begin by dc8 into ring

Change to Oatmeal

Rnd 1 (dc2tog) 4 times (4)
Rnds 2-5 dc (4 rnds)

Do not stuff. Gather remaining stitches to close.

MANE

Working in Camel

Work ch8 CHAIN LOOPS up the back of the neck and head to create a mane (see *Technicals*)

Finish by sewing eyes into place with Black yarn.

LEVEL 3 CAITLIN THE GIRAFFE

ESME
the Fox

Esme is a crafty fox. She makes her own greetings cards, sews, knits and crochets; she'll turn her hand to pretty much anything that involves needles or PVA glue. She has seven children who have an extensive dressing-up box and are always winning school costume competitions. Whether it's for the Nativity, Easter Parade or Halloween, this vixen knows exactly how to throw together the perfect outfit. When she's not threading elastic through headdresses or gluing beads onto shoes she sells her six-shade intarsia tea cosies through an online marketplace.

YARN REQUIRED

75g TOFT DK yarn Fudge
25g TOFT DK yarn Cream

See also: *You Will Need* and *Size Options*.

LEGS (make four)
Work as STANDARD in Fudge

BODY
Work as STANDARD in Fudge

HEAD
Working in Fudge
Work as STANDARD BODY Rnds 1-6
Rnds 7-8 dc (2 rnds)
Rnds 9-11 dc22 Cream, dc20 Fudge (3 rnds)
Rnd 12 dc22 Cream, (dc2tog, dc1) twice, dc2tog, dc4, (dc2tog, dc1) twice, dc2tog Fudge (36)
Rnd 13 dc2tog, dc18, dc2tog Cream, dc14 Fudge (34)
Rnd 14 dc1 Fudge, dc2tog, dc15, dc2tog Cream, dc4, dc2tog, dc3, dc2tog, dc3 Fudge (30)
Rnd 15 dc1 Fudge, dc2tog, dc1, dc2tog, dc7, dc2tog, dc1, dc2tog Cream, dc12 Fudge (26)
Rnd 16 dc2 Fudge, dc12 Cream, (dc2tog, dc2) 3 times Fudge (23)
Rnd 17 dc2tog Fudge, dc21 Cream (22)
Continue in Cream
Rnd 18 (dc4, dc2tog) 3 times, dc2, dc2tog (18)
Rnd 19 (dc4, dc2tog) 3 times (15)
Rnds 20-21 dc (2 rnds)
Rnd 22 (dc1, dc2tog) 5 times (10)
Stuff and gather remaining stitches to close. Using Fudge yarn sew a flash onto head below the colour change.

EARS (make two)
Working in Fudge
Begin by dc6 into ring
Rnd 1 (dc1, dc2 into next st) 3 times (9)
Rnd 2 (dc2, dc2 into next st) 3 times (12)
Rnds 3-4 dc (2 rnds)
Rnd 5 (dc3, dc2 into next st) 3 times (15)

Rnd 6 dc
Rnd 7 (dc4, dc2 into next st) 3 times (18)
Rnd 8 dc
Rnd 9 (dc5, dc2 into next st) 3 times (21)
Rnds 10-11 dc (2 rnds)
Rnd 12 (dc6, dc2 into next st) 3 times (24)
Rnds 13-16 dc (4 rnds)
Rnd 17 (dc2tog) 12 times (12)
Rnd 18 (dc2tog) 6 times (6)
Do not stuff. Gather remaining stitches to close.

TAIL
Working in Fudge
Ch8 and sl st to join into a circle
Rnds 1-4 dc (4 rnds)
Rnd 5 (dc3, dc2 into next st) twice (10)
Rnds 6-8 dc (3 rnds)
Rnd 9 (dc4, dc2 into next st) twice (12)
Rnds 10-12 dc (3 rnds)
Rnd 13 (dc2, dc2 into next st) 4 times (16)
Change to Cream
Rnd 14 (dc3, dc2 into next st) 4 times (20)
Rnds 15-18 dc (4 rnds)
Rnd 19 (dc3, dc2tog) 4 times (16)
Rnd 20 (dc2, dc2tog) 4 times (12)
Rnd 21 (dc2tog) 6 times (6)
Rnd 22 (dc2tog) 3 times (3)
Gather remaining stitches to close then stuff tip and fold flat and sew or dc through both sides of rnd across the top to close.

Finish by sewing eyes and nose into place with Black yarn.

LEVEL 3 ESME THE FOX

BLAKE
the Orangutan

Blake is a self-employed tree surgeon. He has set his pace of life to guarantee that he has plenty of time to smell the roses and steam-mop his slate bathroom floors. This orangutan is a domesticated ape; he cleans, he bakes, and he spends three days a week changing nappies and making purée for his one-year-old twin daughters. Some say he is something of a modern philosopher, pulling insight and truth from his hairy navel as casually as others blow their noses. So when he's not swinging from the treetops or wearing his apron, he's keeping a journal that would be well worth a read.

YARN REQUIRED

75g TOFT DK yarn Fudge
25g TOFT DK yarn Camel

See also: *You Will Need* and *Size Options*.

ARMS (make two)

Work as STANDARD in Camel changing to Fudge after Rnd 2 and working 3cm (1¼in) LOOP STITCH every 3rd st on odd rnds and every 4th st on even rnds then

Rnds 23-30 dc (8 rnds)

LEGS (make two)

Work as STANDARD in Camel changing to Fudge after Rnd 2 and working 3cm (1¼in) LOOP STITCH every 3rd st on odd rnds and every 4th st on even rnds.

BODY

Work as STANDARD in Fudge with 3cm (1¼in) LOOP STITCH every 3rd st on odd rnds and every 4th st on even rnds throughout.

HEAD

Working in Fudge
Work 3cm (1¼in) LOOP STITCH every 3rd st on odd rnds and every 4th st on even rnds
Work as STANDARD BODY Rnds 1-6
Rnds 7-11 dc (5 rnds)
Rnd 12 (dc5, dc2tog) 6 times (36)
Rnd 13 dc
Rnd 14 (dc4, dc2tog) 3 times, dc18 (33)
Rnd 15 (dc3, dc2tog) 3 times, dc18 (30)
Continue without loops
Rnd 16 dc
Rnd 17 (dc3, dc2tog) 6 times (24)
Rnd 18 dc12, (dc1, dc2tog) 4 times (20)
Rnd 19 (dc2, dc2tog) 5 times (15)
Rnd 20 (dc2tog) 7 times, dc1 (8)
Stuff and gather remaining stitches to close.

EARS (make two)

Working in Fudge
Begin by dc6 into ring
Rnd 1 (dc2 into next st) 6 times (12)
Rnds 2-5 dc (4 rnds)
Do not stuff. Gather remaining stitches to close.

FLANGES

Working in Camel
Work as STANDARD BODY Rnds 1-3
Rnd 4 (dc2 into next st) 12 times, dc12 (36)
Rnd 5 (dc3, dc2 into next st) 6 times, dc12 (42)
Rnd 6 (dc2 into next st) 10 times, dc10, (dc2 into next st) 10 times, dc12 (62)
Rnds 7-8 dc (2 rnds)
Rnd 9 dc20, (dc2tog) 5 times, dc20, (dc2tog) 6 times (51)
Rnd 10 dc18, (dc1, dc2tog) 3 times, dc18, (dc2tog) 3 times (45)
Rnds 11-12 dc (2 rnds)
Rnd 13 (dc1, dc2tog) 15 times (30)
Rnd 14 (dc3, dc2tog) 6 times (24)
Rnd 15 (dc2, dc2tog) 6 times (18)
Rnd 16 (dc1, dc2tog) 6 times (12)
Rnd 17 (dc2, dc2tog) 3 times (9)
Sew into position on front of HEAD.

MUZZLE

Working in Camel
Begin by dc6 into ring
Rnd 1 (dc2 into next st) 6 times (12)
Rnd 2 (dc1, dc2 into next st) 6 times (18)
Rnd 3 (dc2, dc2 into next st) 3 times Camel, (dc2, dc2 into next st with 3cm (1¼in) loops every other st) 3 times Fudge (24)
Rnds 4-6 dc12 Camel, dc12 Fudge with 3cm (1¼in) loops every other st (3 rnds)
Continue in Camel without loops
Rnd 7 dc
Stuff and back stitch to sew into position onto bottom of FLANGES.

Finish by sewing eyes and nostrils into place with Black yarn.

LEVEL 3 BLAKE THE ORANGUTAN

HAMLET
the Cheetah

Hamlet is most commonly spotted reflected in your headlights at 6.30pm on your commute home from work. To say that he is addicted to cycling would not be an exaggeration. In fact, he doesn't feel normal unless he's wearing Lycra and his feet are whirring him along faster than 50 miles an hour for at least five of his waking hours every day. He is continually at risk of burning off more calories than he can consume, and so tops himself up with green power shakes and buffalo jerky. He has a complete aversion to towels but loves a long shower, so if you have the rare experience of spotting him off his wheels you can find him at the end of a line of damp paw prints.

YARN REQUIRED

50g TOFT DK yarn Camel
25g TOFT DK yarn Charcoal
25g TOFT DK yarn Cream

See also: *You Will Need* and *Size Options*.

SPOT PATTERN
Working in Camel with 1-st and 2-st spots of Charcoal at random

LEGS (make four)
Work as STANDARD in Camel changing to SPOT PATTERN after Rnd 6

BODY
Work as STANDARD in SPOT PATTERN

HEAD
Working in SPOT PATTERN
Begin by dc6 into ring
Rnd 1 (dc2 into next st) 6 times (12)
Rnd 2 (dc1, dc2 into next st) 6 times (18)
Rnd 3 (dc2, dc2 into next st) 6 times (24)
Rnd 4 (dc3, dc2 into next st) 6 times (30)
Rnd 5 (dc4, dc2 into next st) 6 times (36)
Rnd 6 (dc5, dc2 into next st) 6 times (42)
Rnds 7-11 dc (5 rnds)
Rnd 12 dc10, dc2tog, (dc5, dc2tog) 3 times, dc9 (38)
Rnd 13 dc14, dc2tog, dc6, dc2tog, dc14 (36)
Rnd 14 (dc4, dc2tog) 6 times (30)
Rnd 15 (dc3, dc2tog) 6 times (24)
Rnd 16 dc9, dc2tog, dc2, dc2tog, dc9 (22)
Rnd 17 dc7, dc2tog, dc2, dc2tog, dc9 (20)
Change to Cream
Rnds 18-19 dc (2 rnds)
Rnd 20 (dc2tog) 10 times (10)
Rnd 21 (dc2tog) 5 times (5)
Stuff and gather remaining stitches to close.

EARS (make two)
Working in Cream
Begin by dc6 into ring
Change to Camel
Rnd 1 (dc2 into next st) 6 times (12)
Rnds 2-4 dc (3 rnds)
Rnd 5 dc
Rnd 6 (dc2tog) 6 times (6)
Do not stuff. Gather remaining stitches to close.

TAIL
Working in Charcoal
Begin by dc6 into ring
Rnds 1-6 dc (6 rnds)
Change to SPOT PATTERN
Rnds 7-26 dc (20 rnds)
Do not stuff.

Stitch a border in Black around the muzzle. Finish by sewing eyes and nose into place with Black yarn.

LEVEL 3 HAMLET THE CHEETAH

97

JESSIE
the Raccoon

Jessie is the managing raccoon at the local recycling centre. Obsessed by saving the planet and making this world a greener place through his job, he really wants to make a difference. He is a real dinner-party bore due to his in-depth knowledge of plastic production and the various options for reusing tyres to improve community facilities. He is surely destined for a role on the local council, where he'll be able to meticulously ponder over every seemingly insignificant waste-disposal policy and recommend and influence to his heart's content.

YARN REQUIRED

75g TOFT DK yarn Steel
25g TOFT DK yarn Charcoal
25g TOFT DK yarn Cream

See also: *You Will Need* and *Size Options*.

LEGS (make four)
Work as STANDARD in Steel

BODY
Work as STANDARD in Steel

HEAD
Working in Steel
Begin by dc6 into ring
Rnd 1 (dc2 into next st) 6 times (12)
Rnd 2 (dc1, dc2 into next st) 6 times (18)
Rnd 3 (dc2, dc2 into next st) 6 times (24)
Rnd 4 (dc3, dc2 into next st) 6 times (30)
Rnd 5 (dc4, dc2 into next st) 6 times (36)
Rnd 6 (dc5, dc2 into next st) 6 times (42)
Rnds 7-11 dc (5 rnds)
Rnd 12 (dc5, dc2tog) 6 times (36)
Working LOOP STITCH when instructed
Rnd 13 dc6 with 2cm (¾in) loops, dc6 without loops, dc6 with 2cm (¾in) loops, dc1 with 1.5cm (½in) loop, dc2 with 1cm (⅓in) loops, dc12 without loops, dc2 with 1cm (⅓in) loops, dc1 with 1.5cm (½in) loop (36)
Rnd 14 dc4, dc2tog with 2cm (¾in) loops, dc1 with 1.5cm (½in) loop, dc3, dc2tog, dc1 without loops, dc1 with 1.5cm (½in) loop, dc2, dc2tog, dc4 with 2cm (¾in) loops, dc2tog without loop, (dc4, dc2tog without loops) twice (30)
Continue without loops
Rnd 15 dc16 Steel, dc7 Cream, dc2 Steel, dc5 Cream
Rnd 16 dc2 Cream, dc14 Steel, dc7 Cream, dc3 Steel, dc4 Cream
Rnd 17 dc3 Cream, dc13 Steel, (dc2tog, dc1) 4 times, dc2tog Charcoal (25)
Rnd 18 dc1, dc2tog Charcoal, dc13 Steel, dc3, (dc2tog) twice, dc2 Charcoal (22)
Rnd 19 dc2tog, dc14, (dc2tog) 3 times Charcoal (18)
Rnd 20 dc8 Charcoal, dc10 Cream

Continue in Cream
Rnd 21 dc
Rnd 22 (dc1, dc2tog) 6 times (12)
Rnd 23 (dc2tog) 6 times (6)
Stuff and gather remaining stitches to close.

EARS (make two)
Working in Charcoal
Begin by dc6 into ring
Rnd 1 (dc2 into next st) 6 times (12)
Rnd 2 (dc1, dc2 into next st) 6 times (18)
Rnd 3 dc
Rnd 4 (dc2, dc2 into next st) 6 times (24)
Rnds 5-6 dc (2 rnds)
Do not stuff. Fold flat and sew or dc through both sides of rnd to close.

TAIL
Working in Steel
Work 3cm (1¼in) LOOP STITCH every other st throughout
Ch12 and sl st to join into a circle
Rnds 1-5 dc (5 rnds)
Change to Charcoal
Rnds 6-10 dc (5 rnds)
Change to Steel and continue stripe pattern of 5 rnds Steel, 5 rnds Charcoal
Rnds 11-30 dc (20 rnds)
Continue in Charcoal
Rnd 31 (dc1, dc2tog) 4 times (8)
Do not stuff. Gather tip, fold flat and sew or dc through both sides of rnd to close.

Finish by sewing eyes and nose into place with Black yarn.

LEVEL 3 JESSIE THE RACCOON

NOAH
the Zwartbles Sheep

Noah is a local vicar and borderline saint who tends to his flock more attentively than a ewe does her lambs. In his lifetime he has raised hundreds of thousands for church roofs, children's hospitals and third-world emergency aid. Whether running a marathon dressed as a chicken, having his legs waxed or climbing mountains where only goats dare go, this sheep has done it all in the name of charity. Every year he becomes a gift-giving elf at the local school Christmas fair, and has high hopes to one day swap up to the big red suit.

YARN REQUIRED

75g TOFT DK yarn Charcoal
25g TOFT DK yarn Chestnut
25g TOFT DK yarn Cream

See also: *You Will Need* and *Size Options*.

LEGS (make four)
Work as STANDARD in Charcoal

BODY
Work as STANDARD in Charcoal

HEAD
Working in Charcoal
Begin by dc6 into ring
Rnd 1 (dc2 into next st) 6 times (12)
Rnd 2 (dc1, dc2 into next st) 6 times (18)
Rnd 3 (dc2, dc2 into next st) 6 times (24)
Rnd 4 (dc3, dc2 into next st) 6 times (30)
Rnd 5 (dc4, dc2 into next st) 6 times (36)
Rnd 6 (dc5, dc2 in next st) 6 times (42)
Rnds 7-9 dc8 Cream, dc34 Charcoal (3 rnds)
Rnd 10 dc1 Charcoal, dc7 Cream, dc34 Charcoal
Rnd 11 dc2 Charcoal, dc6 Cream, dc34 Charcoal
Rnd 12 dc2 Charcoal, dc2, dc2tog, dc2 Cream, dc4, dc2tog, (dc5, dc2tog) 4 times Charcoal (36)
Rnds 13-14 dc3 Charcoal, dc4 Cream, dc29 Charcoal (2 rnds)
Rnd 15 dc1, dc2tog Charcoal, dc1, dc2tog, dc1 Cream, dc2tog, dc27 Charcoal (33)
Rnd 16 dc2tog Charcoal, dc2tog, dc1 Cream, dc2tog, dc26 Charcoal (30)
Rnd 17 dc1 Charcoal, dc3 Cream, dc26 Charcoal
Rnd 18 dc1 Charcoal, dc1, dc2tog, dc1 Cream, (dc3, dc2tog) 5 times Charcoal (24)
Rnd 19 dc1 Charcoal, dc23 Cream
Continue in Cream
Rnds 20-21 dc (2 rnds)
Rnd 22 (dc2, dc2tog) 6 times (18)
Rnd 23 dc
Rnd 24 (dc1, dc2tog) 6 times (12)
Rnd 25 (dc2tog) 6 times (6)
Stuff and gather remaining stitches to close.

EARS (make two)
Working in Charcoal
Begin by dc6 into ring
Rnd 1 (dc2 into next st) 6 times (12)
Rnds 2-5 dc (4 rnds)
Rnd 6 (dc2tog) 6 times (6)
Do not stuff. Gather remaining stitches to close.

TAIL
Working in Charcoal
Begin by dc6 into ring
Rnd 1 (dc2 into next st) 6 times (12)
Rnds 2-4 dc (3 rnds)
Rnd 5 (dc2tog) 6 times (6)
Rnd 6 dc
Do not stuff. Gather remaining stitches to close.

FLEECE
Working in Chestnut, work ch8 CHAIN LOOPS all over the body (leave bottom of the body plain to ensure balance when sitting)

Finish by sewing eyes and nose into place with Black yarn.

LEVEL 3 NOAH THE ZWARTBLES SHEEP

CHRISTOPHE
the Wolf

Christophe is nervously awaiting the birth of his first litter of cubs. To onlookers he appears excitedly calm, but internally he is in turmoil and utterly petrified. The more antenatal classes he attends the worse it gets, and he's too scared to read the next chapter of the new dad book he knows he should have completed by now. Despite all his anxiety over the impending life-changing event, everyone around him knows that with his fun-loving nature and big heart he will make the best father any young wolf could hope for.

YARN REQUIRED

75g TOFT DK yarn Steel
25g TOFT DK yarn Cream

See also: *You Will Need* and *Size Options*.

LEGS (make four)
Work as STANDARD in Steel

BODY
Work as STANDARD in Steel

HEAD
Working in Steel
Begin by dc6 into ring
Rnd 1 (dc2 into next st) 6 times (12)
Rnd 2 (dc1, dc2 into next st) 6 times (18)
Rnd 3 (dc2, dc2 into next st) 6 times (24)
Rnd 4 (dc3, dc2 into next st) 6 times (30)
Rnd 5 (dc4, dc2 into next st) 6 times (36)
Rnd 6 (dc5, dc2 into next st) 6 times (42)
Rnds 7-8 dc (2 rnds)
Rnd 9 dc34 Steel, dc8 Cream
Rnd 10 dc18 Cream, dc17 Steel, dc7 Cream
Rnd 11 dc18 Cream, dc18 Steel, dc6 Cream
Rnd 12 dc18 Cream, (dc1, dc2tog) 6 times, dc1 Steel, dc5 Cream (36)
Rnd 13 dc18 Cream, dc15 Steel, dc3 Cream
Rnd 14 (dc4, dc2tog) 3 times Cream, (dc4, dc2tog) twice, dc4 Steel, dc2tog Cream (30)
Rnd 15 dc15 Cream, dc15 Steel
Rnd 16 (dc3, dc2tog) 3 times Cream, (dc3, dc2tog) 3 times Steel (24)
Rnd 17 dc1 Steel, dc11 Cream, dc12 Steel
Rnd 18 dc2 Steel, (dc2tog, dc2) twice, dc2tog Cream, (dc2, dc2tog) 3 times Steel (18)
Continue in Cream
Rnds 19-20 dc (2 rnds)
Rnd 21 (dc1, dc2tog) 6 times (12)
Rnd 22 (dc2, dc2tog) 3 times (9)
Stuff and gather remaining stitches to close.

EARS (make two)
Working in Steel
Begin by dc6 into ring
Rnd 1 (dc1, dc2 into next st) 3 times (9)
Rnd 2 (dc2, dc2 into next st) 3 times (12)
Rnds 3-4 dc (2 rnds)
Rnd 5 (dc3, dc2 into next st) 3 times (15)
Rnd 6 dc
Rnd 7 (dc4, dc2 into next st) 3 times (18)
Rnd 8 dc
Rnd 9 (dc5, dc2 into next st) 3 times (21)
Rnds 10-11 dc (2 rnds)
Rnd 12 (dc6, dc2 into next st) 3 times (24)
Rnds 13-16 dc (4 rnds)
Rnd 17 (dc2tog) 12 times (12)
Rnd 18 (dc2tog) 6 times (6)
Do not stuff. Gather remaining stitches to close.

TAIL
Working in Steel
Ch8 and sl st to join into a circle
Rnds 1-4 dc (4 rnds)
Rnd 5 (dc3, dc2 into next st) twice (10)
Rnds 6-9 dc (4 rnds)
Rnd 10 (dc4, dc2 into next st) twice (12)
Rnds 11-18 dc (8 rnds)
Change to Cream
Rnd 19 (dc5, dc2 into next st) twice (14)
Rnds 20-22 dc (3 rnds)
Rnd 23 (dc2tog) 7 times (7)
Rnd 24 (dc2tog) 3 times, dc1 (4)
Stuff the tip. Fold flat and sew or dc through both sides of rnd across the top to close.

Finish by sewing eyes and nose into place with Black yarn.

LEVEL 3 CHRISTOPHE THE WOLF

NATASHA
the Two-Toed Sloth

Sloth by name but certainly not sloth by nature, Tash has the fastest hands in the West! Known for her head full of red hair (whether straight, curled or styled) and her very big smile, no matter how busy her hands seems she's always got time for a cuppa and a chat about your latest craft project. A beautiful person with a heart of gold, her colleagues sometimes suspect that yarn runs through her veins (soaked in tea of course). If you are ever lucky enough to spot her in the wild – wrapped in a shawl with a turned-up beanie hat and her faithful DMs – you'll never regret stopping to say a 'hello'.

YARN REQUIRED

75g TOFT DK yarn Fudge
25g TOFT DK yarn Cocoa
25g TOFT DK yarn Camel

See also: *You Will Need* and *Size Options*.

LEGS (make four)
Work as STANDARD in Fudge then:
Rnds 23-28 dc (6 rnds)

BODY
Work as STANDARD in Fudge

HEAD
Working in Fudge
Work 4cm (1½in) LOOP STITCH every 3rd st on odd rnds and every 2nd st on even rnds
Begin by dc6 into ring
Rnd 1 (dc2 into next st) 6 times (12)
Rnd 2 (dc1, dc2 into next st) 6 times (18)
Rnd 3 (dc2, dc2 into next st) 6 times (24)
Rnd 4 (dc3, dc2 into next st) 6 times (30)
Rnd 5 (dc4, dc2 into next st) 6 times (36)
Rnd 6 (dc5, dc2 into next st) 6 times (42)
Rnd 7 dc
Continue working 4cm (1½in) LOOP STITCH approx. every 3rd st when instructed
Rnds 8-11 dc29 with loops, dc13 without loops (4 rnds)
Rnd 12 (dc5, dc2tog) 4 times with loops, (dc5, dc2tog) twice without loops (36)
Rnd 13 dc23 with loops, dc13 without loops
Change to Camel and continue without loops
Rnd 14 (dc4, dc2tog) 3 times, dc18 (33)
Rnd 15 (dc3, dc2tog) 3 times, dc18 (30)
Rnd 16 dc
Rnd 17 dc6, (dc2tog, dc1) 8 times (22)
Rnd 18 dc6, (dc1, dc2tog, dc1) 4 times (18)
Rnd 19 (dc4, dc2tog) 3 times (15)
Rnd 20 (dc1, dc2tog) 5 times (10)
Change to Cocoa
Rnd 21 dc
Rnd 22 (dc2tog) 5 times (5)
Stuff and gather remaining stitches to close.

EYES (make two)
Working in Cocoa
Begin by dc6 into ring
Rnd 1 (dc2 into next st) 3 times (incomplete rnd)
Rnd 2 work three 3cm (1¼in) LOOP STITCHES into the next st

CLAWS
Working in Camel
Sl st into position on end of leg
*Ch10, turn and sl st back down chain
SLIP STITCH TRAVERSE 2 sts across foot and repeat from * for second claw
Repeat on the end of each leg.

Finish by cutting loops if desired, and sewing eyes into place with Black yarn.

LEVEL 3 NATASHA THE TWO-TOED SLOTH

NOUSHA
the Persian Cat

Despite her appearance, Nousha actually loves nothing more than rolling her sleeves up and getting stuck in. Whether it's at work with the latest project, at home with a blocked sink, or fundraising for her kittens' school. She's been bringing up her two girls solo since they were in nappies, and is now successfully navigating her way into the teenage years of exams, hormones and the various trends of social media. Juggling as much as anyone can throw at her has become her normality, and so if you need something done, she's your woman.

YARN REQUIRED

100g TOFT DK yarn Cream

See also: *You Will Need* and *Size Options*.

LEGS (make four)

Work as STANDARD in Cream with 2cm (¾in) LOOP STITCH every 3rd st on odd rows and every 4th st on even rows.

BODY

Work as STANDARD in Cream with 3cm (1¼in) LOOP STITCH every 3rd st on odd rows and every 4th st on even rows.

HEAD

Working in LOOP STITCH as body

Begin by dc6 into ring

Rnd 1 (dc2 into next st) 6 times (12)
Rnd 2 (dc1, dc2 into next st) 6 times (18)
Rnd 3 (dc2, dc2 into next st) 6 times (24)
Rnd 4 (dc3, dc2 into next st) 6 times (30)
Rnd 5 (dc4, dc2 into next st) 6 times (36)
Rnd 6 (dc5, dc2 into next st) 6 times (42)
Rnds 7-11 dc (5 rnds)
Rnd 12 (dc5, dc2tog) 6 times (36)
Rnd 13 (dc4, dc2tog) 6 times (30)
Rnd 14 (dc3, dc2tog) 6 times (24)
Rnd 15 dc
Rnd 16 (dc1, dc2tog) 8 times (16)
Rnd 17 (dc2tog) 8 times (8)
Stuff and gather remaining stitches to close.

EARS (make two)

Working in LOOP STITCH as body

Ch10 and sl st to join into a circle

Rnd 1 dc
Rnd 2 (dc2 into next st) 10 times (20)
Rnds 3-4 dc (2 rnds)
Rnd 5 (dc8, dc2tog) twice (18)
Continue without loops
Rnd 6 (dc7, dc2tog) twice (16)
Rnd 7 dc
Rnd 8 (dc6, dc2tog) twice (14)
Rnd 9 (dc5, dc2tog) twice (12)
Rnd 10 (dc4, dc2tog) twice (10)
Rnd 11 (dc3, dc2tog) twice (8)
Rnd 12 (dc2, dc2tog) twice (6)
Do not stuff. Gather remaining stitches to close.

TAIL

Work 2cm (¾in) LOOP STITCH every 4th st throughout

Begin by dc6 into ring

Rnds 1-26 dc (26 rnds)
Do not stuff.

Finish by cutting loops and sewing eyes and nose into place with Black yarn.

LEVEL 3 NOUSHA THE PERSIAN CAT

PERRY
the Guinea Pig

Perry is a very shy guinea pig who likes to stay nestled in the straw every morning for as long as possible. Thankfully he speaks the language of food, and his obsession with slow-roasted barbequing always does the talking (whatever the occasion). Whether midsummer, Mother's Day or even Christmas, he brings out his tongs and lights the coals to bring everyone together. His love of cooking outside in his shorts, sweater or sou'wester has always had the ability to melt any ice and even seems to make people forget that they never see him for breakfast.

YARN REQUIRED

50g TOFT DK yarn Fudge
50g TOFT DK yarn Cream
Length of Stone for nose and mouth

See also: *You Will Need* and *Size Options*.

LEGS (make four)
Work Rnds 1-16 of STANDARD in Cream changing to Fudge for last Rnd.

BODY
Work Rnds 1-14 as STANDARD in Fudge with 3cm (1¼in) LOOP STITCH every 3rd st on odd rnds and every 4th st on even rnds. Work Rnds 15-23 in Cream without loops. Change back to Fudge and LOOP STITCH for Rnds 24-29.

HEAD
Working in Fudge with 3cm (1¼in) LOOP STITCH every 3rd st on odd rnds and every 4th st on even rnds

Begin by dc6 into ring

Rnd 1 (dc2 into next st) 6 times (12)
Rnd 2 (dc1, dc2 into next st) 6 times (18)
Rnd 3 (dc2, dc2 into next st) 6 times (24)
Rnd 4 (dc3, dc2 into next st) 6 times (30)
Rnd 5 (dc4, dc2 into next st) 6 times (36)
Rnd 6 (dc5, dc2 into next st) 6 times (42)
Rnds 7-10 dc (4 rnds)
Rnd 11 dc5, dc2tog without loops, (dc5, dc2tog) 5 times with loops (36)
Rnd 12 dc6 without loops, dc30 with loops
Rnd 13 dc4, dc2tog without loops, (dc4, dc2tog) 5 times with loops (30)
Rnd 14 (dc2tog) 3 times without loops, dc24 with loops (27)
Continue without loops
Rnd 15 (dc2tog, dc7) 3 times (24)
Change to Cream
Rnd 16 dc
Rnd 17 (dc2, dc2tog) 6 times (18)
Rnd 18 (dc4, dc2tog) 3 times (15)
Rnd 19 (dc1, dc2tog) 5 times (10)
Stuff and gather remaining stitches to close.

FLASH
Working in Cream
Ch5 and work in rows as follows:
Rows 1-3 dc4, turn (3 rows)
Row 4 dc2 into next st, dc2, dc2 into next st, turn (6)
Rows 5-6 dc6, turn (2 rows)
Row 7 dc2 into next st, dc4, dc2 into next st, turn (8)
Rows 8-9 dc8, turn (2 rows)
Sew into position on head.

EARS
Working in Fudge
Begin by dc6 into ring
Rnd 1 (dc2 into next at) 6 times (12)
Rnd 2 (dc1, dc2 into next st) 6 times (18)
Rnds 3-4 dc (2 rnds)
Do not stuff. Gather remaining stitches to close.

Finish by cutting and trimming loops, and sewing eyes into place with Black yarn and nose and mouth with Stone yarn.

LEVEL 3 PERRY THE GUINEA PIG

109

CYBIL
the Sugar Glider

Cybil is the kind of party guest you have to escort to bed just before the sun rises, which usually happens to be exactly the time when she's about to reveal the most exciting stories in her repertoire. One of the most entertaining chatterboxes you'll ever come across, it's a mystery to most how she finds the time to draw a breath and learn all about half the things she talks about in between telling everyone else about them. The theory is she's found a way to avoid ever needing shut-eye, so she's got all day to hide inside devouring every book, play and film she can find, and then once the moon comes out she's got all night long to re-live them.

YARN REQUIRED

100g TOFT DK yarn Silver
25g TOFT DK yarn Charcoal
25g TOFT DK yarn Cream
25g TOFT DK yarn Oatmeal

See also: *You Will Need* and *Size Options*.

LEGS (make four)
Work as STANDARD in Silver

BODY
Work as STANDARD in Silver

HEAD
Working in Silver
Work as STANDARD BODY Rnds 1-6
Rnd 7 dc8 Silver, dc5 Charcoal, dc29 Silver
Rnd 8 dc9 Silver, dc5 Charcoal, dc18 Silver, dc10 Cream
Rnd 9 dc9 Cream, dc5 Charcoal, dc28 Cream
Rnds 10-11 dc10 Cream, dc5 Charcoal, dc27 Cream (2 rnds)
Rnd 12 dc2, dc2tog, (dc1, dc2tog) twice, dc1 Cream, dc4 Charcoal, (dc1, dc2tog) 3 times, dc18 Cream (36)
Rnd 13 dc5, dc2tog, dc1 Cream, dc1, dc2tog, dc1 Charcoal, dc1, dc2tog, dc21 Cream (33)
Rnd 14 dc8 Cream, dc2 Charcoal, dc8, (dc2tog, dc1) 5 times Cream (28)
Rnd 15 (dc2tog, dc1) twice, dc2 Cream, dc1 Charcoal, dc3, (dc2tog, dc1) twice, dc10 Cream (24)
Rnd 16 (dc2tog, dc2) 6 times Cream (18)
Rnd 17 (dc1, dc2tog) 3 times, dc8 Cream, dc1 Charcoal (15)
Rnd 18 dc15 Charcoal
Change to Oatmeal
Rnd 19 (dc3, dc2tog) 3 times (12)
Rnd 20 dc
Rnd 21 (dc2, dc2tog) 3 times (9)
Stuff and gather remaining stitches to close.

EARS (make two)
Working in Charcoal
Ch10 and sl st to join into a circle
Rnd 1 dc
Rnd 2 (dc2 into next st, dc4) twice (12)
Rnd 3 (dc3, dc2 into next st) 3 times (15)
Rnds 4-7 dc (4 rnds)
Change to Oatmeal
Rnds 8-9 dc (2 rnds)
Rnd 10 (dc1, dc2tog) 5 times (10)
Rnd 11 (dc2tog) 5 times (5)
Do not stuff. Gather remaining stitches to close.

BACK STRIPE
Working in Charcoal
Ch32, turn and work back down ch as follows:
Row 1 miss 2 sts, tr30
Sew into position with the end joining the colour changing pattern on the head.

TAIL
Working in Charcoal
Begin by dc6 into ring
Rnd 1 (dc2 into next st) 6 times (12)
Rnd 2 (dc3, dc2 into next st) 3 times (15)
Rnds 3-10 dc (8 rnds)
Rnd 11 (dc3, dc2tog) 3 times (12)
Change to Silver
Rnds 12-36 dc (25 rnds)
Stuff the tip. Fold flat and sew or dc through both sides of rnd across the top to close.

PATAGIA (make two)
Working in Silver
Once stuffed and sewn together, SLIP STITCH TRAVERSE 21 sts along one side of body between front and back legs
Work back and forth along these 21 sts as follows:
Rows 1-15 dc21, sl st 1 into leg, turn (15 rows)

Finish by sewing eyes into place with Black yarn.

LEVEL 3 CYBIL THE SUGAR GLIDER

NOEL
the Chipmunk

Self-employed since he decided not to walk into his final exam at school, he could never be accused of not having worked very hard for what he's got. He suits his yellow hard hat and high-vis so much that some speculate he was born wearing them! Never happier than sitting on a digger breaking ground on a new project, he's a traditional kind of bloke whose greatest desire is to build houses that people will still be living in 200 years from now.

YARN REQUIRED

75g TOFT DK yarn Stone
25g TOFT DK yarn Cream
25g TOFT DK yarn Charcoal

See also: *You Will Need* and *Size Options*.

LEGS (make four)
Work as STANDARD in Stone

BODY
Work as STANDARD in Stone

HEAD
Working in Stone
Work as STANDARD BODY Rnds 1-6

Rnd 7 dc14 Stone, (dc6, dc2 into next st) 3 times, dc7 Cream (45)

Rnd 8 dc14 Stone, (dc7, dc2 into next st) 3 times, dc7 Cream (48)

Rnd 9 dc14 Stone, dc34 Cream

Rnds 10-11 dc1 Cream, dc13 Stone, dc34 Cream

Rnd 12 dc2 Cream, dc12 Stone, dc34 Cream

Rnd 13 dc2tog Cream, (dc1, dc2tog) 4 times Stone, dc1, dc2tog, dc31 Cream (42)

Rnd 14 dc2 Cream, dc2, dc2tog, dc2 Stone, dc2tog, dc1, dc2tog, dc20, (dc2tog, dc1) 3 times Cream (36)

Rnd 15 dc2 Cream, dc5 Stone, dc10, (dc2tog) 5 times, dc9 Cream (31)

Rnd 16 dc3 Cream, dc4 Stone, (dc2tog) 3 times, dc12, (dc2tog) 3 times Cream (25)

Rnd 17 dc4 Cream, dc3 Stone, dc4, dc2tog, dc3, (dc2tog) twice, dc3, dc2tog Cream (21)

Rnd 18 dc1, dc2tog, dc2 Cream, dc2 Stone, dc2, dc2tog, dc1 (dc2tog, dc1) 3 times Cream (16)

Rnd 19 (dc2tog) twice Cream, dc2 Stone, (dc2tog) twice, dc6 Cream (12)

Rnd 20 dc2tog Cream, dc2, dc2tog, dc6 Stone (10)

Rnd 21 (dc2tog) 5 times Stone (5)

Stuff and gather remaining stitches to close.

EYE PATCHES (make two)
Working in Cream
Begin by dc6 into ring
Rnd 1 (dc1, dc2 into next st) 3 times (9)
Do not stuff.

FACE STRIPES (make two)
Working in Charcoal, ch15, turn and sl st back down chain, ch15 and sl st back down chain.

EARS (make two)
Working in Stone
Begin by dc6 into ring
Rnd 1 (dc2 into next st) 6 times (12)
Rnd 2 dc
Rnd 3 (dc3, dc2 into next st) 3 times (15)
Rnd 4 dc
Do not stuff. Gather remaining stitches to close.

BACK STRIPES
Working in Charcoal, ch23 then turn and dc22 sts to create 8 rows of stripes in the following order: Charcoal, Cream, Charcoal, Stone, Stone, Charcoal, Cream, Charcoal.

TAIL
Working in Stone
Work 2cm (¾in) LOOP STITCH every other st in Stone and every st in Charcoal
Ch12 and sl st to join into a circle
Rnds 1-4 dc2 Stone, dc1 Charcoal, dc9 Stone (4 rnds)
Rnds 5-8 dc3 Stone, dc1 Charcoal, dc8 Stone (4 rnds)
Rnds 9-12 dc4 Stone, dc1 Charcoal, dc7 Stone (4 rnds)
Rnds 13-16 dc5 Stone, dc1 Charcoal, dc6 Stone (4 rnds)
Rnds 17-20 dc6 Stone, dc1 Charcoal, dc5 Stone (4 rnds)
Rnds 21-24 dc7 Stone, dc1 Charcoal, dc4 Stone (4 rnds)
Rnds 25-28 dc8 Stone, dc1 Charcoal, dc3 Stone (4 rnds)
Continue in Stone
Rnd 29 (dc2tog) 6 times (6)
Do not stuff. Gather remaining stitches to close.

Align back stripes with back of neck and attach by sewing all the way round the piece. Sew face stripes along the edge of the central colour section on face from ears to centre of face and then across cheeks. Sew eye patches into position.

Finish by sewing eyes and nose into place with Black yarn.

LEVEL 3 NOEL THE CHIPMUNK

113

GINA
the Hyena

Gina's beside herself plucking up the courage to propose. She's planned a grand holiday with a setting and a date, but has got a shiny ring really burning a hole in her pocket. All she needs is a proper shot at a romantic moment without a phone in anyone's hand, kids around and before anyone falls asleep on the sofa. A new plan's emerging closer to home involving a fish and chip supper, a flask of tea and a sunset. Although, she hasn't got a clue how to predict one of those glorious pink-sky nights rather than a grey drizzly Monday. Here's hoping that's tomorrow.

YARN REQUIRED

75g TOFT DK yarn Stone
25g TOFT DK yarn Cocoa

See also: *You Will Need* and *Size Options*.

LEGS (make four)

Working in Stone

Begin by dc6 into ring

Rnd 1 (dc2 into next st) 6 times (12)

Rnd 2 (dc1, dc2 into next st) 6 times (18)

Rnds 3-6 dc (4 rnds)

Rnd 7 (dc1, dc2tog) 6 times (12)

Rnd 8 dc3 Stone, dc3 Cocoa, dc6 Stone

Rnd 9 dc Stone

Rnd 10 dc9 Stone, dc3 Cocoa

Rnd 11 dc Stone

Rnd 12 dc3 Stone, dc4 Cocoa, dc5 Stone

Rnd 13 dc Stone

Rnd 14 dc7 Stone, dc5 Cocoa

Rnds 15-16 dc Stone (2 rnds)

Rnd 17 dc6 Cocoa, dc6 Stone

Rnd 18 dc Stone

Rnd 19 dc6 Stone, dc6 Cocoa

Rnd 20 dc Stone

Rnd 21 dc1 Stone, dc6 Cocoa, dc5 Stone

Rnd 22 dc Stone

Stuff end and sew flat across top to close.

BODY

Working in Stone

Begin by dc6 into ring

Rnd 1 (dc2 into next st) 6 times (12)

Rnd 2 (dc1, dc2 into next st) twice Stone, (dc1, dc2 into next st) 3 times Cocoa, dc1, dc2 into next st Stone (18)

Rnd 3 (dc2, dc2 into next st) 6 times Stone (24)

Rnd 4 (dc3, dc2 into next st) twice Cocoa, (dc3, dc2 into next st) 4 times Stone (30)

Rnd 5 (dc4, dc2 into next st) 3 times Stone, (dc4, dc2 into next st) 3 times Cocoa (36)

Rnd 6 dc5, dc2 into next st Stone, dc5, dc2 into next st Cocoa, dc3, dc2 into next st, (dc5, dc2 into next st) 3 times Stone (42)

Rnd 7 (dc6, dc2 into next st) twice, dc3 Stone, dc3, dc2 into next st, dc3 Cocoa, dc3, dc2 into next st, (dc6, dc2 into next st) twice Stone (48)

Work 2cm (¾in) LOOP STITCH every st when instructed

Rnd 8 dc8 Cocoa, dc14, dc1 loop Stone, dc2 loops Cocoa, dc1 loop, dc4 Stone, dc8 Cocoa, dc10 Stone

Rnd 9 dc12 Stone, dc10 Cocoa, dc1 loop Stone, dc2 loops Cocoa, dc1 loop, dc22 Stone

Rnd 10 dc15 Stone, dc7 Cocoa, dc1 loop Stone, dc2 loops Cocoa, dc1 loop Stone, dc10 Cocoa, dc12 Stone

Continue working 3cm (1¼in) LOOP STITCH every st when instructed

Rnd 11 dc22, dc1 loop Stone, dc2 loop Cocoa, dc1 loop Stone, dc15 Cocoa, dc7 Stone

Rnd 12 dc9 Stone, dc13 Cocoa, dc1, dc1 loop Stone, dc2 loops Cocoa, dc1 loop, dc21 Stone

Rnd 13 dc2tog, dc4, dc2tog, dc5 Stone, dc10 Cocoa, dc1 loop Stone, dc2 loops Cocoa, dc1 loop Stone, dc6 Cocoa, dc9, dc2tog, dc4 Stone (45)

Rnd 14 dc21, dc1 loop Stone, dc2 loops Cocoa, dc1 loop Stone, dc11 Cocoa, dc9 Stone

Rnd 15 (dc1, dc2tog) 5 times Stone, (dc1, dc2tog) twice Cocoa, dc1 loop Stone, dc2tog with loop Cocoa, dc1 loop, dc2tog, (dc1, dc2tog) 6 times Stone (30)

Rnd 16 dc8 Stone, dc7 Cocoa, dc1 loop Stone, dc1 loop Cocoa, dc1 loop Stone, dc8 Cocoa, dc4 Stone

LEVEL 3 GINA THE HYENA

115

Rnd 17 dc15, dc1 loop Stone, dc1 loop Cocoa, dc1 loop Stone, dc6 Cocoa, dc6 Stone

Rnd 18 dc15, dc1 loop Stone, dc1 loop Cocoa, dc1 loop, dc12 Stone

Rnd 19 dc6 Stone, dc9 Cocoa, dc1 loop Stone, dc1 loop Cocoa, dc1 loop, dc12 Stone

Rnd 20 dc11 Stone, dc4 Cocoa, dc1 loop Stone, dc1 loop Cocoa, dc1 loop Stone, dc9 Cocoa, dc3 Stone

Continue working 4cm (1½in) LOOP STITCH every st when instructed

Rnd 21 (dc3, dc2tog) 3 times, dc3 loops, dc2tog with loop, (dc3, dc2tog) twice Stone (24)

Rnd 22 dc8 Stone, dc4 Cocoa, dc4 loops Stone, dc4 Cocoa, dc4 Stone

Rnd 23 dc12, dc4 loops, dc8 Stone

Rnd 24 dc8 Stone, dc4 Cocoa, dc1, dc4 loops Stone, dc5 Cocoa, dc2 Stone

Rnd 25 dc10 Stone, dc2 Cocoa, dc4 loops, dc8 Stone

Rnd 26 dc12, dc4 loops Stone, dc5 Cocoa, dc3 Stone

Rnd 27 (dc2, dc2tog) twice Stone, dc2 dc2tog Cocoa, dc2 loops, dc2tog with loops, (dc2, dc2tog) twice Stone (18)

Continue in Stone

Rnd 28 dc10 Stone, dc3 loops, dc5 Stone

Rnd 29 (dc2tog) 9 times Stone (9)

HEAD

Working in Stone

Work 2cm (¾in) LOOP STITCH every st when instructed

Begin by dc6 into ring making a loop on the 2nd and 5th st

Rnd 1 dc2 into next st, dc2 loops into next st, (dc2 into next st) twice, dc2 loops into next st, dc2 into next st (12)

Rnd 2 dc1, dc2 into next st, dc1, dc2 loops into next st, (dc1, dc2 into next st) twice, dc1, dc2 loops into next st, dc1, dc2 into next st (18)

Rnd 3 dc2, dc2 into next st, dc2, dc2 loops into next st, (dc2, dc2 into next st) twice, dc2, dc2 loops into next st, dc2, dc2 into next st (24)

Rnd 4 dc3, dc2 into next st, dc3, dc2 loops into next st, (dc3, dc2 into next st) twice, dc3, dc2 loops into next st, dc3, dc2 into next st (30)

Rnd 5 dc4, dc2 into next st, dc4, dc2 loops into next st, (dc4, dc2 into next st) twice, dc4, dc2 loops into next st, dc4, dc2 into next st (36)

Rnd 6 dc5, dc2 into next st, dc5, dc2 loops into next st, (dc5, dc2 into next st) twice, dc5, dc2 loops into next st, dc5, dc2 into next st (42)

Rnds 7-8 dc13, dc2 loops, dc27 (2 rnds)

Rnds 9-10 dc14, dc2 loops, dc26 (2 rnds)

Continue without loops

Rnd 11 dc

Rnd 12 (dc5, dc2tog) 6 times (36)

Rnd 13 dc5, (dc2tog, dc1) 6 times, dc13 (30)

Rnd 14 dc

Rnd 15 dc6, (dc2tog) 6 times, dc12 (24)

Change to Cocoa

Rnd 16 (dc4, dc2tog) 4 times (20)

Rnd 17 dc

Rnd 18 (dc3, dc2tog) 4 times (16)

Rnd 19 dc

Rnd 20 dc2tog, dc10, (dc2tog) twice (13)

Rnd 21 dc11, dc2tog (12)

Stuff and gather remaining stitches to close.

EARS (make two)

Working in Stone

Ch12 and sl st to join into a circle

Rnd 1 dc

Rnd 2 (dc3, dc2 into next st) 3 times (15)

Change to Cocoa

Rnd 3 dc

Change to Stone

Rnd 4 dc

Change to Cocoa

Rnd 5 (dc4, dc2 into next st) 3 times (18)

Rnds 6-7 dc (2 rnds)

Rnd 8 dc6, (dc2tog) 3 times, dc6 (15)

Rnd 9 dc4, (dc2tog) 3 times, dc5 (12)

Rnd 10 (dc2tog) 6 times (6)

Do not stuff. Gather remaining stitches to close.

TAIL

Working in Stone

Work 2cm (¾in) LOOP STITCH every 3rd st

Ch8 and sl st to join into a circle

Rnds 1-8 dc (8 rnds)

Rnd 9 dc2tog, dc6 (7)

Rnd 10 dc

Continue working 4cm (1½in) LOOP STITCH every other st

Rnd 11 dc2tog, dc5 (6)

Rnds 12-17 dc (6 rnds)

Rnd 18 dc2tog, dc4 (5)

Change to Cocoa and work 4cm (1½in) LOOP STITCH every 3rd st

Rnds 19-22 dc (4 rnds)

Do not stuff. Gather remaining stitches to close.

Finish by sewing eyes and nose into place with Black yarn.

LEVEL 3 GINA THE HYENA

ANDREA
the Ocelot

Andrea's an ocelot you're lucky to ever really catch sight of (let alone have a chance to admire her spots). Declaring she was born nocturnal and endlessly told off at school for napping on her desk, she finally found her rhythm years ago on her first week of night shifts and has never felt better. However, it's a mystery what it is she does by night. Some say they've seen her in a uniform, others say she's got tell-tale white handprints on an apron in the morning, and there's one over-friendly neighbour who claims to have spotted her boot open once and it was loaded with amps and cables. Who knows?

YARN REQUIRED

25g TOFT DK yarn Cream
50g TOFT DK yarn Oatmeal
25g TOFT DK yarn Camel
25g TOFT DK yarn Charcoal

See also: *You Will Need* and *Size Options*.

LEGS (make four)

Work Rnds 1-5 as STANDARD in Cream

Rnd 6 (dc5 Cream, dc1 Charcoal) 3 times

Rnd 7 (dc1, dc2tog) 6 times Cream (12)

Rnd 8 (dc2 Cream, dc1 Charcoal, dc1 Cream) 3 times

Rnd 9 dc Cream

Rnd 10 (dc1 Charcoal, dc1 Oatmeal, dc2 Cream) 3 times

Rnd 11 dc Cream

Rnd 12 (dc1 Oatmeal, dc1 Cream, dc1 Charcoal, dc1 Oatmeal) 3 times

Rnd 13 dc Oatmeal

Rnd 14 (dc1 Charcoal, dc3 Oatmeal) 3 times

Rnd 15 dc Oatmeal

Rnds 16-17 (dc2 Oatmeal, dc1 Charcoal, dc1 Oatmeal) 3 times (2 rnds)

Rnd 18 dc Oatmeal

Rnds 19-21 (dc1 Charcoal, dc2 Oatmeal) 4 times (3 rnds)

Rnd 22 dc Oatmeal

BODY

Work Rnds 1-7 as STANDARD in Oatmeal

Rnd 8 dc1 Charcoal, dc4 Oatmeal, dc1 Charcoal, dc1 Oatmeal, dc1 Charcoal, dc5 Oatmeal, dc1 Charcoal, dc2 Oatmeal, dc1 Charcoal, dc2 Oatmeal, dc1 Charcoal, dc3 Oatmeal, dc1 Charcoal, dc24 Oatmeal

Rnd 9 dc Oatmeal

Rnd 10 dc3 Oatmeal, dc1 Camel, dc1 Charcoal, dc4 Oatmeal, dc1 Charcoal, dc1 Camel, dc1 Charcoal, dc3 Oatmeal, dc1 Camel, dc1 Charcoal, dc4 Oatmeal, dc1 Charcoal, dc1 Camel, dc1 Charcoal, dc24 Oatmeal

Rnd 11 dc3 Oatmeal, dc2 Charcoal, dc2 Oatmeal, dc1 Charcoal, dc2 Oatmeal, dc1 Charcoal, dc4 Oatmeal, dc2 Charcoal, dc2 Oatmeal, dc1 Charcoal, dc2 Oatmeal, dc2 Charcoal, dc24 Oatmeal

Rnd 12 dc1 Charcoal, dc11 Oatmeal, dc1 Camel, dc1 Charcoal, dc5 Oatmeal, dc1 Camel, dc1 Charcoal, dc27 Oatmeal

Rnd 13 dc2 Oatmeal, dc1 Camel, dc1 Charcoal, dc3 Oatmeal, dc1 Charcoal, dc2 Camel, dc2 Oatmeal, dc2 Charcoal, dc3 Oatmeal, dc1 Charcoal, dc5 Oatmeal, dc1 Charcoal, dc6, (dc2tog, dc4) 3 times Oatmeal (45)

Rnd 14 dc2 Oatmeal, dc2 Charcoal, dc3 Oatmeal, dc2 Charcoal, dc1 Camel, dc6 Oatmeal, dc1 Charcoal, dc2 Camel, dc3 Oatmeal, dc2 Charcoal, dc21 Oatmeal

Rnd 15 (dc1, dc2tog) 4 times Oatmeal, dc1 Charcoal, dc2tog, dc1 Oatmeal, dc2tog Charcoal, dc1, dc2tog Oatmeal, dc1, dc2tog Camel, (dc1, dc2tog) 7 times Oatmeal (30)

Rnd 16 dc2 Oatmeal, dc1 Charcoal, dc1 Camel, dc4 Oatmeal, dc1 Charcoal, dc1 Camel, dc4 Oatmeal, dc1 Charcoal, dc15 Oatmeal

Rnd 17 dc2 Oatmeal, dc1 Charcoal, dc1 Camel, dc2 Oatmeal, dc1 Camel, dc1 Oatmeal, dc1 Charcoal, dc1 Camel, dc3 Oatmeal, dc1 Camel, dc1 Charcoal, dc2 Oatmeal, dc1 Charcoal, dc12 Oatmeal

Rnd 18 dc2 Oatmeal, dc1 Charcoal, dc1 Camel, dc1 Oatmeal, dc1 Charcoal, dc1 Camel, dc2 Oatmeal, dc1 Charcoal, dc1 Camel, dc2 Oatmeal, dc1 Camel, dc1 Charcoal, dc1 Oatmeal, dc1 Camel, dc1 Charcoal, dc12 Oatmeal

Rnd 19 dc3 Oatmeal, dc1 Charcoal, dc2 Oatmeal, dc1 Charcoal, dc2 Oatmeal, dc1 Charcoal, dc1 Camel, dc3 Oatmeal, dc1 Charcoal, dc1 Oatmeal, dc1 Camel, dc1 Charcoal, dc12 Oatmeal

Rnd 20 dc2 Oatmeal, dc1 Charcoal, dc7 Oatmeal, dc1 Charcoal, dc5 Oatmeal, dc1 Camel, dc1 Charcoal, dc12 Oatmeal

Rnd 21 dc2 Oatmeal, dc1 Charcoal, dc2tog Oatmeal, dc1 Charcoal, dc2, dc2tog Oatmeal, dc2 Oatmeal, dc1 Charcoal, dc2tog, (dc3, dc2tog) 3 times Oatmeal (24)

LEVEL 3 ANDREA THE OCELOT

Rnd 22 dc1 Oatmeal, dc1 Camel, dc1 Charcoal, dc1 Oatmeal, dc1 Charcoal, dc1 Oatmeal, dc1 Charcoal, dc1 Camel, dc1 Charcoal, dc1 Oatmeal, dc1 Charcoal, dc2 Oatmeal, dc1 Charcoal, dc10 Oatmeal

Rnd 23 dc1 Oatmeal, dc2 Camel, dc3 Oatmeal, dc1 Charcoal, dc1 Camel, dc1 Charcoal, dc3 Oatmeal, dc1 Camel, dc1 Charcoal, dc10 Oatmeal

Rnd 24 dc2 Oatmeal, dc1 Charcoal, dc3 Oatmeal, dc1 Charcoal, dc1 Camel, dc1 Charcoal, dc3 Oatmeal, dc1 Camel, dc1 Charcoal, dc10 Oatmeal

Rnd 25 dc Oatmeal

Rnd 26 dc4 Oatmeal, dc1 Charcoal, dc3 Oatmeal, dc1 Charcoal, dc2 Oatmeal, dc1 Charcoal, dc12 Oatmeal

Rnd 27 dc2, dc2tog Oatmeal, dc1 Charcoal, dc1, dc2tog, (dc2, dc2tog) 4 times Oatmeal (18)

Continue in Oatmeal

Rnd 28 dc

Rnd 29 (dc2tog) 9 times (9)

HEAD

Working in Oatmeal

Begin by dc6 into ring

Rnd 1 (dc1 Oatmeal, dc1 into the same st Charcoal, dc2 into next st Oatmeal) 3 times (12)

Rnd 2 (dc1, dc2 into next st) 6 times Oatmeal (18)

Rnd 3 (dc1 Charcoal, dc1, dc2 into next st, dc2, dc2 into next st Oatmeal) 3 times (24)

Rnd 4 (dc1 Charcoal, dc2, dc2 into next st, dc3, dc2 into next st Oatmeal) 3 times (30)

Rnd 5 (dc4, dc2 into next st) 6 times Oatmeal (36)

Rnd 6 (dc1 Charcoal, dc2 Oatmeal, dc1 Charcoal, dc1 Oatmeal, dc2 into next st Charcoal, dc3 Oatmeal, dc1 Charcoal, dc1, dc2 into next st Oatmeal) 3 times (42)

Rnd 7 (dc1 Charcoal, dc2 Oatmeal, dc1 Charcoal, dc6 Oatmeal, dc1 Charcoal, dc3 Oatmeal) 3 times

Rnd 8 dc Oatmeal

Rnd 9 dc7 Oatmeal, dc1 Charcoal, dc2 Oatmeal, dc1 Charcoal, dc10 Oatmeal, dc1 Charcoal, dc4 Oatmeal, dc1 Charcoal, dc9 Oatmeal, dc1 Charcoal, dc4 Oatmeal, dc1 Charcoal

Rnd 10 dc21 Oatmeal, dc1 Charcoal, dc4 Oatmeal, dc1 Charcoal, dc9 Oatmeal, dc1 Charcoal, dc4 Oatmeal, dc1 Charcoal

Rnd 11 dc6 Oatmeal, dc1 Charcoal, dc3 Oatmeal, dc1 Charcoal, dc3 Oatmeal, dc1 Charcoal, dc6 Oatmeal, dc1 Charcoal, dc4 Oatmeal, dc1 Charcoal, dc9 Oatmeal, dc1 Charcoal, dc4 Oatmeal, dc1 Charcoal

Rnd 12 dc6 Oatmeal, dc1 Charcoal, dc7 Oatmeal, dc1 Charcoal, dc6 Oatmeal, dc1 Charcoal, dc4 Oatmeal, dc1 Charcoal, dc9 Oatmeal, dc1 Charcoal, dc4 Oatmeal, dc1 Charcoal

Rnd 13 dc4, dc2tog Oatmeal, dc1 Charcoal, dc2tog, dc3, dc2tog Oatmeal, dc1 Charcoal, dc2tog, dc25 Oatmeal (38)

Rnd 14 dc2tog, dc3 Oatmeal, dc1 Charcoal, dc5 Oatmeal, dc1 Charcoal, dc3, dc2tog, dc21 Oatmeal (36)

Rnd 15 dc4 Oatmeal, dc1 Charcoal, dc2tog, dc3 Oatmeal, dc1 Charcoal, dc2tog, (dc4, dc2tog) 3 times, dc3, dc2tog Oatmeal (30)

Rnd 16 dc4 Oatmeal, dc1 Charcoal, dc1, dc2tog Oatmeal, dc1 Charcoal, dc2, dc2tog, (dc1, dc2tog, dc1) 4 times Cream (24)

Rnd 17 dc4 Cream, dc1 Charcoal, dc3 Oatmeal, dc1 Charcoal, dc15 Cream

Rnd 18 dc3, dc2tog Cream, dc3 Oatmeal, dc2tog, dc2, dc2tog, dc6, dc2tog, dc2 Cream (20)

Continue in Cream

Rnds 19-20 dc (2 rnds)

Rnd 21 (dc2tog) 10 times (10)

Rnd 22 (dc2tog) 5 times (5)

Stuff and gather remaining stitches to close.

EARS (make two)

Working in Cream

Begin by dc6 into ring

Rnd 1 (dc2 into next st) 6 times (12)

Rnd 2 (dc3, dc2 into next st) 3 times (15)

Rnds 3-4 dc (2 rnds)

Change to Oatmeal

Rnds 5-6 dc (2 rnds)

Do not stuff. Sew or dc through both sides of rnd to close. Fold flat and dc around the curved edge in Charcoal.

TAIL

Working in Charcoal

Begin by dc8 into ring

Continue working 4 rounds Charcoal, 4 rounds Oatmeal

Rnds 1-28 dc (28 rnds)

Change to Oatmeal

Rnds 29-36 dc (8 rnds)

Do not stuff.

Sew triangle nose into place using Black yarn and then fill in by sewing with Camel yarn.

Finish by sewing eyes into place with Black yarn.

LEVEL 3 ANDREA THE OCELOT

SAVANNA
the African Painted Dog

A seamstress that's only happy when her machine is whizzing away hemming her latest creation. Always ears to toe in a self-made outfit, Savanna's wardrobe is bursting with bold pattern, colour and metres of flowing cotton. It's not just about never feeling like shop-bought clothes fit her properly, she gets such an incredible sense of pride when she turn heads with her own style of clashing patterns and curving shapes.

YARN REQUIRED

50g TOFT DK yarn Camel
25g TOFT DK yarn Charcoal
25g TOFT DK yarn Cream

See also: *You Will Need* and *Size Options*.

LEGS (make four)

Working in Charcoal

Begin by dc6 into ring

Rnd 1 (dc2 into next st) 6 times (12)

Rnd 2 (dc1, dc2 into next st) 6 times (18)

Rnd 3 dc2 Charcoal, dc4 Cream, dc1 Charcoal, dc3 Cream, dc3 Charcoal, dc5 Cream

Rnd 4 dc3 Charcoal, dc2 Cream, dc3 Charcoal, dc3 Cream, dc1 Charcoal, dc6 Cream

Rnd 5 dc2 Charcoal, dc3 Cream, dc4 Charcoal, dc5 Cream, dc2 Charcoal, dc2 Cream

Rnd 6 dc1 Charcoal, dc5 Cream, dc2 Charcoal, dc6 Cream, dc2 Charcoal, dc2 Cream

Rnd 7 (dc1, dc2tog) twice Cream, dc1 Charcoal, dc2tog, dc1, dc2tog, dc1 Cream, dc2tog, dc1, dc2tog Charcoal (12)

Rnds 8-10 (dc1 Charcoal, dc3 Cream) twice, dc1 Cream, dc3 Charcoal (3 rnds)

Rnd 11 dc1 Charcoal, dc7 Cream, dc1 Charcoal, dc3 Cream

Continue in Cream

Rnds 12-18 dc (7 rnds)

Change to Camel

Rnds 19-22 dc (4 rnds)

Stuff end and sew flat across top to close.

BODY

Begin by dc6 into ring

Rnd 1 (dc2 into next st) 6 times (12)

Rnd 2 (dc1, dc2 into next st) 6 times (18)

Rnd 3 dc2, dc2 into next st Camel, dc2, dc2 into next st Charcoal, (dc2, dc2 into next st) 4 times Camel (24)

Rnd 4 dc3 Camel, dc2 into next st Charcoal, dc3, dc2 into next st Charcoal, (dc3, dc2 into next st) twice Camel, dc3, dc2 into next st Charcoal, dc3, dc2 into next st Camel (30)

Rnd 5 dc4, dc2 into next st Camel, dc4 Cream, dc2 into next st Charcoal, (dc4, dc2 into next st) twice Camel, dc4 Cream, dc2 into next st Charcoal, dc4, dc2 into next st Camel (36)

Rnd 6 dc5, dc2 into next st, dc1 Camel, dc4, dc2 into next st, dc2 Charcoal, dc3, dc2 into next st, dc5 Camel, dc2 into next st, dc4 Cream, dc1, dc2 into next st Charcoal, dc4 Camel, dc1, dc2 into next st Charcoal (42)

Rnd 7 dc3 Charcoal, dc3, dc2 into next st, dc1 Camel, dc2 Charcoal, dc3, dc2 into next st, dc3 Cream, dc3, dc2 into next st, dc6, dc2 into next st Camel, dc4 Cream, dc2 Charcoal, dc2 into next st, dc4 Camel, dc2, dc2 into next st Charcoal (48)

Rnd 8 dc4 Cream, dc6 Camel, dc5 Charcoal, dc4 Cream, dc12 Camel, dc2 Charcoal, dc3 Cream, dc2 Charcoal, dc8 Camel, dc2 Charcoal

Rnd 9 dc5 Cream, dc7 Camel, dc5 Charcoal, dc14 Camel, dc5 Charcoal, dc12 Camel

Rnd 10 dc5 Charcoal, dc5 Camel, dc6 Cream, dc1 Charcoal, dc31 Camel

Rnd 11 dc10 Camel, dc6 Cream, dc2 Charcoal, dc16 Camel, dc6 Charcoal, dc4 Camel, dc4 Charcoal

Rnd 12 dc3 Charcoal, dc10 Camel, dc4 Charcoal, dc17 Camel, dc1 Charcoal, dc4 Cream, dc5 Camel, dc4 Charcoal

Rnd 13 dc1 Charcoal, dc4 Cream, dc9 Camel, (dc4, dc2tog) 3 times Camel, dc2 Camel, dc1 Charcoal, dc4 Cream, dc5 Camel, dc4 Cream (45)

Rnd 14 dc4 Charcoal, dc6 Camel, dc5 Charcoal, dc16 Camel, dc1 Charcoal, dc5 Cream, dc4 Camel, dc4 Charcoal

LEVEL 3 SAVANNA THE AFRICAN PAINTED DOG

Rnd 15 dc1, dc2tog Charcoal, (dc1, dc2tog) twice Camel, (dc1, dc2tog) 3 times Charcoal, (dc1, dc2tog) 4 times Camel, (dc1, dc2tog) twice, dc1 Charcoal, dc2tog, dc1, dc2tog Camel, dc1, dc2tog Charcoal (30)

Rnd 16 dc4 Charcoal, dc2 Camel, dc1 Charcoal, dc5 Cream, dc11 Camel, dc2 Charcoal, dc5 Camel

Rnd 17 dc1 Camel, dc4 Cream, dc1 Camel, dc1 Charcoal, dc5 Cream, dc1 Charcoal, dc16 Camel, dc1 Charcoal

Rnd 18 dc3 Charcoal, dc5 Camel, dc5 Charcoal, dc16 Camel, dc1 Charcoal

Rnd 19 dc1 Charcoal, dc22 Camel, dc4 Charcoal, dc3 Camel

Rnd 20 dc23 Camel, dc2 Cream, dc4 Charcoal, dc1 Camel

Rnd 21 (dc3, dc2tog) 4 times, dc3 Camel, dc2tog Cream, dc3, dc2tog Charcoal (24)

Rnd 22 dc19 Camel, dc5 Charcoal

Rnd 23 dc1 Charcoal, dc2 Camel, dc6 Charcoal, dc15 Camel

Rnd 24 dc3 Camel, dc4 Cream, dc2 Charcoal, dc15 Camel

Rnd 25 dc2 Camel, dc8 Charcoal, dc14 Camel

Continue in Camel

Rnd 26 dc

Rnd 27 (dc2, dc2tog) 6 times (18)

Rnd 28 dc

Rnd 29 (dc2tog) 9 times (9)

HEAD

Working in Camel

Begin by dc6 into ring

Rnd 1 (dc2 into next st) 6 times (12)

Rnd 2 (dc1, dc2 into next st) 6 times (18)

Rnd 3 (dc2, dc2 into next st) 6 times (24)

Rnd 4 (dc3, dc2 into next st) 6 times (30)

Rnd 5 (dc4, dc2 into next st) 6 times (36)

Rnd 6 (dc5, dc2 into next st) 6 times (42)

Rnds 7-8 dc2 Camel, dc3 Charcoal, dc37 Camel (2 rnds)

Rnds 9-10 dc3 Camel, dc3 Charcoal, dc36 Camel (2 rnds)

Rnd 11 dc4 Camel, dc2 Charcoal, dc36 Camel

Rnd 12 dc2tog, dc2 Camel, dc2 Charcoal, dc1, (dc2tog, dc5) 5 times Camel (36)

Rnds 13-14 dc4 Camel, dc1 Charcoal, dc31 Camel (2 rnds)

Continue in Camel

Rnd 15 (dc1, dc2tog) 5 times, dc18 dc1, dc2tog (30)

Rnd 16 dc

Rnd 17 (dc2tog) 5 times, dc9 Camel, dc9, dc2tog Charcoal (24)

Continue in Charcoal

Rnds 18-20 dc (3 rnds)

Rnd 21 (dc2, dc2tog) 6 times (18)

Rnd 22 (dc1, dc2tog) 6 times (12)

Rnd 23 (dc2, dc2tog) 3 times (9)

Stuff and gather remaining stitches to close.

EARS (make two)

Working in Charcoal

Begin by dc6 into ring

Rnd 1 (dc2 into next st) 6 times (12)

Rnd 2 (dc1, dc2 into next st) 6 times (18)

Rnd 3 (dc2, dc2 into next st) 6 times (24)

Rnd 4 (dc3, dc2 into next st) 6 times (30)

Rnds 5-10 dc (6 rnds)

Change to Cream

Rnd 11 (dc3, dc2tog) 6 times (24)

Rnd 12 dc

Rnd 13 (dc2, dc2tog) 6 times (18)

Manipulate fabric to move coloured section to bottom centre of ear. Sew flat across edges to close. Sew into position.

TAIL

Working in Camel

Ch10 and sl st to join into a circle

Rnds 1-5 dc (5 rnds)

Change to Charcoal

Rnd 6 (dc1, dc2 into next st) 5 times (15)

Change to Cream and work 2cm (¾in) LOOP STITCH every 3rd st on odd rnds and every 4th st on even rnds

Rnds 7-21 dc (15 rnds)

Rnd 22 (dc1, dc2tog) 5 times (10)

Rnd 23 (dc2tog) 5 times (5)

Stuff lightly. Fold flat and sew or dc through both sides of rnd across the top to close.

Finish by sewing eyes and nose into place with Black yarn.

LEVEL 3 SAVANNA THE AFRICAN PAINTED DOG

JANE
the Pangolin

By the time the beginning of Advent comes around, Jane is just about ready to hang up her glittery festive boots and curl up into a ball until the new year. She's declared this Christmas a zero-waste year in her household, and items can only be wrapped or boxed in something usefully reusable. Under the guise of sustainability she's planning on a relaxing November and December without any of the usual stresses of choosing a colour scheme and matching every bow and ribbon to it.

YARN REQUIRED

75g TOFT DK yarn Camel
Length of Mushroom for nose

See also: *You Will Need* and *Size Options*.

BODY

Work as STANDARD in Camel

HEAD

Begin by dc6 into ring
Rnd 1 (dc2 into next st) 6 times (12)
Rnd 2 (dc1, dc2 into next st) 6 times (18)
Rnd 3 (dc2, dc2 into next st) 6 times (24)
Rnd 4 (dc3, dc2 into next st) 6 times (30)
Rnd 5 (dc4, dc2 into next st) 6 times (36)
Rnds 6-10 dc (5 rnds)
Rnd 11 (dc1, dc2tog) 6 times, dc18 (30)
Rnds 12-13 dc (2 rnds)
Rnd 14 (dc3, dc2tog) 6 times (24)
Rnds 15-16 dc (2 rnds)
Rnd 17 (dc2, dc2tog) 6 times (18)
Rnds 18-19 dc (2 rnds)
Rnd 20 dc2, dc2tog, dc2, dc2tog, dc10 (16)
Rnds 21-22 dc (2 rnds)
Rnd 23 (dc2, dc2tog) 4 times (12)
Rnd 24 (dc2tog) 3 times, dc6 (9)
Stuff and gather remaining stitches to close.

EARS (make two)

Begin by dc6 into ring
Rnd 1 (dc2 into next st) 6 times (12)
Rnds 2-3 dc (2 rnds)
Do not stuff. Gather remaining stitches to close.

BACK LEGS (make two)

Work as STANDARD in Camel

FRONT LEGS (make two)

Refer to PANGOLIN SCALES (*Technicals: Additional Techniques*)

Begin by dc6 into ring
Rnd 1 (dc2 into next st) 6 times (12)
Rnd 2 (dc1, dc2 into next st) 6 times (18)
Rnds 3-6 dc (4 rnds)
Rnd 7 (dc1, dc2tog) 6 times (12)
Rnds 8-9 dc (2 rnds)
Stuff end and dc5 across both edges to close, then continue as follows:
Row 1 ch2 (counts as first tr), tr1 into first st on leg, ch1, miss one st, tr1 into next st, ch1, miss one st, tr2 into next st (the two trebles together at either end are referred to as 'twin posts')
Row 2 make 2 scales around twin posts
Row 3: Decrease Setup
sl st into centre of last scale, ch4, tr1 into space between the scales on one side of the post, then tr1 into space on other side of post, ch1, tr1 into centre of next scale across
Row 4 make 1 scale around twin posts
Row 5: Increase Setup
sl st into top right of scale below, ch2 (counts as first tr), miss 2 ch and tr1 into base of ch, ch1, tr1 into centre of scale below, ch1, tr2 into top left of scale below
Row 6 make 2 scales
Row 7 decrease setup
Row 8 make 1 scale

LEVEL 3 JANE THE PANGOLIN

ARMOUR

Refer to PANGOLIN SCALES (*Technicals: Additional Techniques*)

Starting with one scale at tip of tail

Row 1 ch7, tr2 in fifth ch from hook, ch1, tr1 into last ch

Row 2 make 1 scale around twin posts

Row 3: Increase Setup

sl st into top right of scale below, ch2 (counts as first tr), miss 2 ch and tr1 into base of ch, ch1, tr1 into centre of scale below, ch1, tr2 into top left of scale below

Row 4 make 2 scales around twin posts

Row 5: Decrease Setup

sl st into centre of last scale, ch4, tr1 into space between the scales on one side of the post, then tr1 into space on other side of post, ch1, tr1 into centre of next scale across

Row 6 make 1 scale

Rows 7-26 repeat Rows 3-6 five times (20 rows)

Row 27 increase setup

Row 28 make 2 scales

Row 29 increase setup with one extra repeat

Row 30 make 3 scales

Row 31 increase setup with two extra repeats

Row 32 make 4 scales

Row 33 increase setup with three extra repeats

Row 34 make 5 scales

Row 35 decrease setup with three extra repeats

Row 36 make 4 scales

Row 37 increase setup with three extra repeats

Row 38 make 5 scales

Row 39 decrease setup with three extra repeats

Row 40 make 4 scales

Row 41 decrease setup with two extra repeats

Row 42 make 3 scales

Row 43 increase setup with two extra repeats

Row 44 make 4 scales

Row 45 decrease setup with two extra repeats

Row 46 make 3 scales

Row 47 decrease setup with one extra repeat

Row 48 make 2 scales

Row 49 increase setup with one extra repeat

Row 50 make 3 scales

Row 51 decrease setup with one extra repeat

Row 52 make 2 scales

Row 53 increase setup with one extra repeat

Row 54 make 3 scales

Row 55 decrease setup with one extra repeat

Row 56 make 2 scales

Attach armour to head and body after stuffing and sewing up body, head and ears. Start by sewing final two scales to top of head between ears, the first row of five scales should line up with the bottom of body, and then oversew around the edge of the piece. Sew on legs last.

Finish by sewing eyes into place with Black yarn and nose with Mushroom yarn.

LEVEL 3 JANE THE PANGOLIN

TECHNICALS

In the following pages I aim to equip a complete beginner with the skills to make any or all of the menagerie animals. Even if you are a seasoned crocheter, take the time to glance over the instructions as specific techniques to this style of crochet, such as decreasing and colour changing, may be new to you.

BASIC SKILLS

HOLDING YOUR HOOK

When learning to crochet you need to find a position of holding your hook and yarn that's most comfortable for you. There's no right or wrong way, but generally speaking choose between a knife or pencil hold in your dominant hand for your hook, and hold the yarn in your other hand in a way that makes it easy to wrap it around the hook while holding the crochet piece between your thumb and middle finger.

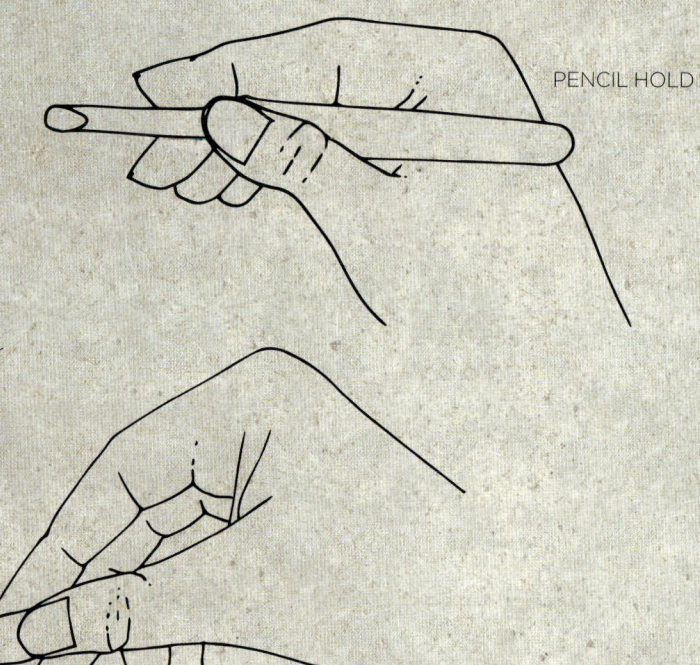

PENCIL HOLD

KNIFE HOLD

RIGHT SIDE AND WRONG SIDE OF FABRIC

Another essential skill is learning to recognise the right side (RS) from the wrong side (WS) of the fabric. You should always be pushing the hook into the fabric from the outside to the inside, and whether you are left handed or right handed the next stitch you are working should always be closest to your body with the part you are making on the other side. It is a very easy mistake to work an animal inside out, and although on the Level 1 animals this is not a problem and you can flip them the other way before sewing up, this will not be possible on the more advanced ones.

RS   WS

MARKING

Use a stitch marker to keep track of the end of each round as you work. I recommend tying in a piece of contrast yarn approximately 15cm (6in) long after the end of Rnd 1 (12 sts); as you get back around to it, pull it forwards or backwards over your stitches to weave a marker up your fabric. The marker can be removed when finished.

ABBREVIATIONS

ch: Chain. A chain is the most fundamental of all crochet stitches.

dc: Double crochet. Using the double crochet stitch creates a compact and dense fabric. (NB: This is known as sc – single crochet – in US terminology.)

dc2tog: Double crochet two stitches together (decrease by one stitch).

Rnd: Round. A round is a complete rotation in a spiral back to your stitch marker. With these patterns you DO NOT slip stitch at the end of a round to make a circle, but instead continue straight onto the next round in a spiral.

Row: Rows create a flat piece of fabric rather than working in spirals. When working a row turn and work immediately back into the stitch you've just worked to keep the same number of stitches on each rows.

RS: Right side. The right side of your fabric will show small 'V' shapes in horizontal lines and will form the outside of the animal.

sl st: Slip stitch. This is the simplest crochet stitch.

st(s): Stitch(es). You can count your stitches around the edge of your fabric.

tr: Treble. A longer more open stitch than the double crochet. (NB: This is known as dc – double crochet – in US terminology.)

WS: Wrong side. The wrong side of your fabric will have vertical spiraling furrows. This is where you have all the ends or strands of yarn, and it forms the inside of the animal.

WORKING THE STITCHES

SLIP KNOT

1. Make a loop in the yarn.
2. Pull the yarn through the loop. 
3. Place your hook through the loop and tighten. 

CHAIN

1. With your slip knot on your hook, wrap yarn over the hook (yarn over).
2. Twist the hook downwards and pull the yarn through the loop. 
3. Repeat until desired length. 

NB: US crocheters will know this stitch as single crochet (sc).

DOUBLE CROCHET

1. Insert the hook through the stitch under both loops of the 'V'.
2. Yarn over and pull through the stitch (two loops on hook). 
3. Yarn over again and pull through both loops to end with one loop.

FOUNDATION RING (DC6 INTO RING)

1. Make a slip knot and chain two stitches, then insert the hook into the first chain stitch.

2. Work a double crochet stitch into this stitch.

3. Work five more double crochet stitches into this same stitch to make six stitches in total. Pull tightly on the tail of the yarn to close the centre of the ring and form a neat circle.

SLIP STITCH TO JOIN INTO CIRCLE

1. Chain the number of stitches stated, then insert the hook into the stitch closest to the slip knot.

2. Yarn over hook, pull the yarn through the stitch and loop on the hook in one motion.

3. Work the first stitch of the round into the last chain that you made.

NB: Some of the pattern instructions require a dc3tog or dc4tog. Work these decreases using the same method but through the stated number of stitches together.

DECREASE (DC2TOG)

1. Insert the hook through the front loop of the stitch only (two loops on the hook).

2. Insert the hook through the front loop of the next stitch (three loops on the hook).

3. Yarn over hook and pull through first two loops on the hook, then yarn over and through both remaining loops to complete the double crochet.

TECHNICALS WORKING THE STITCHES

133

NB. On a rnd with more than one colour the colour the stitches should be worked in always follows the instruction.

CHANGING COLOUR

1. On your last stitch before the colour change. Insert the hook through the next stitch, yarn over and pull through the stitch (two loops on hook).

2. Yarn over with the new colour and complete the double crochet stitch with this new yarn.

3. Continue with this new colour, leaving the original colour to the back of the work. Cut if a one-off colour change or run on the WS of the fabric if colour changing back to it.

LOOP STITCH

1. Insert the hook through the stitch, wrap the yarn from front to back around your thumb, yarn over and pull through the stitch.

2. Pull the loop to the front and to length stated in the pattern, then yarn over and pull through the two loops on hook to complete the stitch.

3. Repeat to work loops as often as stated in the pattern. Measure loops from the fabric to the end of the loop.

SLIP STITCH TRAVERSE

1. Insert the hook into the fabric around a stitch and yarn over.

2. Pull through the fabric and loop in one motion.

3. Continue moving across the fabric like this to reach the desired location or number stated in the pattern.

FINISHING TECHNIQUES

CHAIN LOOPS

1. Insert the hook into the fabric around a stitch, yarn over and pull through the fabric.

2. Chain the number of stitches stated in the pattern, then insert hook into the fabric approx. 2 stitches and 2 rows away. Yarn over and pull through the fabric.

3. Repeat step 2 until the area is covered.

SLIP STITCH CHAINS

1. Insert the hook into the fabric around a stitch, yarn over and pull through the fabric.

2. Chain the number of stitches stated in the pattern.

3. Slip stitch back down the chain and then slip stitch into the fabric. Repeat as instructed.

CHAIN TAIL

1. Fold the yarn to create a piece approx. 20cm (8in) long that is four strands thick. Insert the hook through into the fabric around a stitch and yarn over, pulling all four strands through the loop.

2. Loosely chain the number of stitches stated in the pattern.

3. Into the final stitch work further chains using a single strand of yarn creating loops as stated.

TECHNICALS WORKING THE STITCHES / FINISHING TECHNIQUES

135

ADDITIONAL TECHNIQUES

NB: US crocheters will know this stitch as double crochet (dc).

TREBLE CROCHET

1. Yarn over and insert the hook into the stitch.

2. Yarn over and pull through the stitch (three loops on hook), yarn over and pull through first two loops on hook.

3. Yarn over and pull through remaining two loops on hook.

PANGOLIN SCALES

MAKING A SCALE

1. Without turning, tr5 around the first post of the twin post, ch1

2. tr5 around the second post of the twin post to complete the scale

DECREASE SETUP

1. sl st into the centre of last scale, ch4

2. tr1 into space between the scales on one side of the post, then tr1 into space on other side of post, ch1 and tr into centre of next scale across

INCREASE SETUP

1. sl st into top right of scale below, ch2, miss 2 chains and tr1 into base of chain, ch1

2. tr1 into centre of scale below, ch1, tr2 into top left of scale below

TOPKNOTS AND TAILS

Don't be afraid of pinching and stitching the parts to add shape to an ear or tail before sewing into position as this will create expression and character.

TECHNICALS ADDITIONAL TECHNIQUES / TOPKNOTS AND TAILS

STUFFING AND SEWING

When stuffing your animal remember that you want to show off its shape, but don't want to make it too firm and hard. Much of the appeal with this collection comes from the drape of the body, which is created through a combination of the luxury yarn and light-handed stuffing. Once you have crocheted the pieces and pushed the stuffing into them, you will need to roll and manipulate the pieces in your hands to spread the stuffing evenly and ensure the best shape.

STUFFING THE BODIES

All the bodies are stuffed. With the long-necked animals, be aware that you will need to make the bodies slightly firmer to ensure they hold their heads up straight.

STUFFING THE HEADS

All the heads are stuffed once complete unless otherwise instructed in the pattern. The instructions for stuffing any other pieces such as horns will be detailed in the individual patterns.

FINISHING THE EARS

The ears are not stuffed; see *Face Details* for advice on positioning them.

FINISHING THE FEET AND LEGS

What gives *Edward's Menagerie* its unique appeal is the stuffing method of padding out the animals' feet but leaving their legs hollow and flat. In order for the animals to sit up on your mantlepiece, nursery shelf or dashboard, you need to splay the legs and sew them on the lines that divide the bottom into thirds. This will ensure that the animals will balance forwards onto their tummies.

STUFFING THE TAILS

The instructions for stuffing the tails are detailed in the individual patterns. They are all attached in the same location on the back centre body, and identifying this place is made easier if you do it last and sit them up.

ORDER OF SEWING

1. Sew on the head with two stitches between the top of the body and under the head. Then oversew around these stitches in a small circle between the two parts to secure.
2. Sew the front legs to the top of the body.
3. Sew the back legs to the bottom of the body in a splayed position.
4. Sew on the ears and add any facial details.
5. Sew the tail into position.
6. Add any further details such as fleece or mane if required.

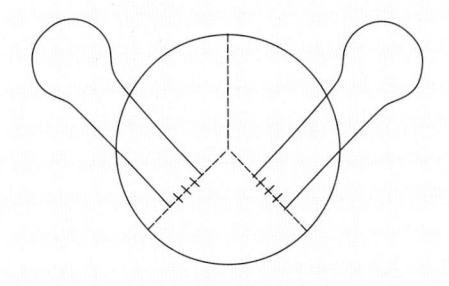

BACK LEG POSITION

TECHNICALS STUFFING AND SEWING

139

FACE DETAILS

Sewing on the face details is when your animal's personality really begins to emerge. Take your time to get this right; don't be afraid to cut it all off and start again (I do this frequently when working on a new animal).

SEWING ON EARS

Unless otherwise detailed in the individual pattern instructions, you will create more character by pinching together the bottom of an ear before stitching it in place on the head.

POSITIONING THE EARS

The position of the ears can portray the mood of the animal. Placing them to the side of the head and pointing forwards and down will give a sad and sleepy appearance. Conversely, placing them high on the top of the head will suggest that the animal is surprised or alert, so there is often a balance somewhere in between the two. The most important factor is to get the two ears evenly placed, so mark the central stitch at the top of the head and count out from there along the same row.

SEWING ON EYES

When sewing the eyes I have used a simple method of wraps of yarn running vertically through the same stitches across rows. Using more wraps to create bigger eyes will make the animal look cuter and younger.

SEWING ON NOSES

The noses vary significantly from animal to animal. Some just have simple nostrils; others have large triangular noses with the suggestion of a mouth, and others have none at all. You could use the same overdyed black thread that you are using for the eyes, although using a lighter shade of yarn on the nose can often give the animal 'softness'; this is used to great effect in certain animals such as *Emma the Bunny*.

When making nostrils, vertically oversew around one stitch. The distance you choose to separate the nostrils will help shape the character of your animal. In the case of animals with dark faces you may want to use a lighter yarn to add detail.

SEWING ON EYES

1. Secure the black yarn at the top of the eye position.
2. Sew into the fabric two rounds up and back down into the original hole. 
3. Repeat three times. Fasten off ends. 

SEWING ON NOSES

1. Secure yarn in top left nose position. 
2. Sew through top right nose position down into the middle and pull yarn tight, ensuring needle is on top of thread to make a 'V' shape. 
3. Secure yarn with a single stitch, or continue to sew additional features such as filling in the nose or adding a mouth.

WASHING

If made in natural yarn and stuffed with synthetic stuffing material, the animals can either be washed by hand or on a gentle cold machine cycle. Please be aware that if you opt to use natural stuffing sponge the surface clean for the best results.

SAFETY

Your animal will only be as safe as you make it, so don't skimp on the stitches when sewing up. With ears and legs, I oversew all the way around the edges – you really can't sew them too much! I have also only used yarn to sew on eyes. You could use beads or buttons as an alternative. Never use toy safety eyes, beads or buttons on an animal intended for a child under three years old; you should embroider the details instead.

TECHNICALS FACE DETAILS, WASHING AND SAFETY

THANK YOU

Thanks to Edward Lord, born 2012, and to my daughter Alexandra born four years later for all the inspiration and daily feedback on what I'm crocheting.

The patterns and projects in these books have been developed, remade and tested by so many hands over the last decade that it's impossible to list everyone here.

A specific thank you to TOFT team members Natasha Jackson for her speedy hook and Rachel Critchley for her sharp attention to detail and to the TOFT creative team Rosie Collins, Beth Plumbley and Yantra Taneva for making everything look so beautiful.

Wider thanks are due to the TOFT team (past and present) who work hard everyday to deliver TOFT products around the world, and help our customers learn to crochet and enjoy the craft as much as we do. Working alongside a group of such creative and talented people is an honour.

Without the support of my family I could not continue to run an expanding business.

Thank you to Ame Verso and David and Charles for letting my revisit this very special book a decade on and divulge everything I have learned teaching people to crochet in that time.

A final thanks to all the *Edward's Menagerie* fans out there who continue to support TOFT. Your passion for my designs and our yarns keeps me crocheting as fast as I can!

SUPPLIERS

All TOFT yarns can be purchased direct from www.toftuk.com

For international stockists of TOFT yarns see website for details.

INDEX

Aardvark, Winston the 42-3
abbreviations 131
African painted dog, Savanna the 122-5
antlers 86-7
arms 40, 44, 94

Bat, Clarence the 74-5
boards 66, 72
bears
   Penelope the 50-1
   Piotr the Polar 22-3
   William the Sloth 82-3
Bison, Isaac the American 46-7
bodies 82, 90, 94, 106, 114-24
   standard 15
   stuffing 138

Caribou, Caspar the Peary 86-7
cats
   Alexandre the Russian Blue 20-1
   Nousha the Persian 106-7
chain loops 135
chain stitch 131, 132
chain tails 135
Cheetah, Hamlet the 96-7
Chimpanzee, Benedict the 40-1
Chipmunk, Noel the 112-13
claws 104
colour 10
   changes 134
counting stitches 14
cows
   Douglas the Highland 58-9
   Sarah the Friesian 88

decrease (dc2tog) 131, 133
dogs
   Milo the 28-9
   Savanna the African painted 122-5

Donkey, Angharad the 56-7
double crochet stitch 131, 132

ears
   finishing 138
   Level 1 18-46
   Level 2 50-66, 70-6
   Level 3 80-92, 96-102, 106-8, 112, 120, 124-6
   positioning 140
   sewing on 140
Elephant, Bridget the 24-5
eye patches 40, 44
eyes 54, 104, 140-1

fabric, right/wrong side of 130-1
faces 10, 112, 140
feet 138
finishing techniques 135
flanges 94
flashes 108
fleece 36, 52, 100
foundation rings 133
Fox, Esme the 92-3

Giraffe, Caitlin the 90-1
Goat, Audrey the Nanny 66-7
Gorilla, Germaine the 44-5
Guinea Pig, Perry the 108-9

hair 44
heads
   Level 1 18-46
   Level 2 50-66, 70-6
   Level 3 80-112, 116, 120, 124-6, 138
Hedgehog, Francis the 76-7
Hippo, Georgina the 30-1
hooks, holding 130
horns 32, 46, 58, 66, 72
Hyena, Gina the 114-17

Koala, Samuel the 80-1

legs
   finishing 138
   Level 1 24, 30, 32
   Level 2 74, 96
   Level 3 90, 94, 104-8, 114, 118, 122, 126
   standard 15
Level 1 projects 16-47
Level 2 projects 48-77
Level 3 projects 78-129
Lion, Rufus the 38-9
loop stitch 78, 134

manes 38, 46, 56, 62, 64, 72, 90
marking 131
muzzles 40, 44, 94

noses 26, 30, 140, 141

Ocelot, Andrea the 118-21
Orangutan, Blake the 94-5
ossicones 90

Panda, Fiona the 54-5
Pangolin, Jane the 126-9, 136
Pig, Richard the Large White 26-7
Polar Bear, Piotr the 22-3
Pony, Chardonnay the Palomino 62-3

rabbits
   Beth the Dutch 68-9
   Emma the Bunny 18-19
Raccoon, Jessie the 98-9
Rhino, Austin the 32-3

safety issues 141
Sea Otter, Andrew the 70-1
sewing 138, 140
sheep
   Hank the Dorset Down 52-3
   Noah the Zwartbles 100-1
   Simon the 36-7

size options 12-13
slip knots 132
slip stiches 131
slip stitch chains 135
slip stitch to join into circle 133
slip stitch traverse 134
Sloth, Natasha the Two-Toed 104-5
Sloth Bear, William the 82-3
spines 76
spot patterns 96
Squirrel, Bradlee the Grey 84-5
standard forms 14-15
stitch counting 14
stitch working 132-4
stripes 64, 110, 112
stuffing 10, 138
Sugar Glider, Cybil the 110-11

tails 137
   Level 1 18-38, 42, 46
   Level 2 50-66, 70-72
   Level 3 82-92, 96-102, 106, 110-12, 116, 120, 124
   stuffing 138
technicals 130-41
terminology 13
Tiger, Laurence the 60-1
topknots 58, 137
treble crochet 131, 136

Wallaby, Karl the 34-5
washing toys 141
Wildebeest, Owen the 72-3
wings 74
Wolf, Christophe the 102-3

yarn 10, 12-13

Zebra, Alice the 64-5

143

A DAVID AND CHARLES BOOK
© David and Charles, Ltd 2024

David and Charles is an imprint of David and Charles, Ltd
Suite A, Tourism House, Pynes Hill, Exeter, EX2 5WS

Text and Designs © Kerry Lord 2014, 2024
Layout and Photography © Kerry Lord and David and Charles, Ltd 2014, 2024

First published in the UK and USA in 2014

This edition first published in 2024

Kerry Lord has asserted her right to be identified as author of this work in accordance with the Copyright, Designs and Patents Act, 1988.

All rights reserved. No part of this publication may be reproduced in any form or by any means, electronic or mechanical, by photocopying, recording or otherwise, without prior permission in writing from the publisher.

Readers are permitted to reproduce any of the designs in this book for their personal use and without the prior permission of the publisher. However, the designs in this book are copyright and must not be reproduced for resale.

The author and publisher have made every effort to ensure that all the instructions in the book are accurate and safe, and therefore cannot accept liability for any resulting injury, damage or loss to persons or property, however it may arise.

Names of manufacturers and product ranges are provided for the information of readers, with no intention to infringe copyright or trademarks.

A catalogue record for this book is available from the British Library.

ISBN-13: 9781446310625 paperback
ISBN-13: 9781446313541 hardback
ISBN-13: 9781446312025 EPUB

This book has been printed on paper from approved suppliers and made from pulp from sustainable sources.

FSC® C012521 — MIX Paper from responsible sources

Printed in China through Asia Pacific Offset for:
David and Charles, Ltd
Suite A, Tourism House, Pynes Hill, Exeter, EX2 5WS

10 9 8 7 6 5 4 3 2 1

Publishing Director: Ame Verso
Managing Editor: Jeni Chown
Technical Editor: Rachel Critchley
Head of Design: Anna Wade
Lead Designer: Rosie Collins
Photographer: Yantra Taneva
Stylist: Beth Plumbley
Illustrator: Evelyn Birch
Pre-press Designer: Susan Reansbury
Production Manager: Beverley Richardson

David and Charles publishes high-quality books on a wide range of subjects. For more information visit www.davidandcharles.com.

Share your makes with us on social media using #dandcbooks and follow us on Facebook and Instagram by searching for @dandcbooks.

Layout of the digital edition of this book may vary depending on reader hardware and display settings.